Reins on my Life

Joe Crews

AMAZING FACTS

First Edition Published in 1977
Second Edition Published in 1986

Published by
Amazing Facts, Inc.
PO Box 1058
Roseville, CA 95678-8058

Cover Design by
Haley Trimmer

Layout by
Greg Solie - Altamont Graphics

ISBN # 1-58019-059-6

Table of Contents

Foreword 4
1. Brush with Death 5
2. Sixteen and Uncertain 10
3. College Romance and Narrow Escape 19
4. Angel in My Tent 25
5. Calamities and Comedies 31
6. A Tithing Miracle 39
7. Double Trouble at the Bus Stop 45
8. Baby Boys and Stormy Weather 52
9. Introduction to India 58
10. Veiled Trouble and Mistaken for a King 65
11. Attacked by a Hindu Mob 73
12. Government Orders, "Get Out!" 82
13. Pakistan Tragedy 91
14. Adventures in Moslem Evangelism 97
15. From Karachi to Texas 104
16. Brain Tumor! Test of Faith 113
17. Preachers in Doubt 120
18. Venture in Radio 123
19. Surgery by God 131
20. No Survivors 136
Epilogue 141

Foreword

This book has been reluctantly written by my friend, Joe Crews, in response to many urgent requests. The reticence stemmed from recognition of the fact that books written in the first person often inadvertently appear to put erring human beings in the limelight

Though this book involves the life of Joe Crews, it is really a record of the thrilling providential intervention of the Master in Joe's life, and its purpose is to bring honor and glory to the lovely name of our Lord and to help hasten the finishing of His work in the earth. To this end the Amazing Facts Board sends it forth. May the Spirit of God rest upon you as you read it, and may it play at least some small part in preparing you for the return of Jesus is my heartfelt hope.

—Bill May, Former Chairman
Amazing Facts Board of Directors

1
Brush With Death

Colfax, North Carolina, in the year of my birth, was a tiny crossroads community midway between Greensboro and Winston-Salem. It straddled the main dirt highway, State No. 421, which provided the only road connection between those two bustling cities. Colfax consisted mainly of a post office, a railroad station and a big public school which joined my father's farm only a quarter mile from the big frame house where I was born. There was also a Wesleyan Methodist campground a mile further up the road, which attracted hundreds of earnest, shouting, evangelical Christians during the ten-day summer camp meeting. Colfax was almost seriously described as located between the third and fourth signs of a Burma Shave advertisement.

The first sixteen years of my life revolved around the people and events of that little Tarheel community. It was there that the greatest decision of my life was made—when I accepted Christ as my Saviour. The marvel of God's grace in finding me there among the tobacco rows, and calling me to be a minister, is the subject of this book. It is not going to be the usual kind of conversion story. I have no dramatic recital of sinful escapades, drug addiction or wild youth flings. I would not glorify them by the telling even if they had occurred.

Too often youth have been stirred by the exciting lurid description of sinful living, and scarcely remember a word about the joy of deliverance. That is not to say that I was a saint. Far from it. No other human heart but my own will ever know some of the secret battles against self and sin that were waged during those sixteen years. But the point is, they were not extraordinary, and I was nothing more than an awkward, unattractive little boy in an obscure rural community. This is the very point which makes my conversion so remarkable. Nobody paid any particular attention to me outside my home. Why did God seek me out? I still stand in awe when I think of His love for a poor, fumbling lad in country overalls. But God seems to delight in taking the most hopeless materials and transforming them into vessels of honor. Oh, the riches of His grace!

God does not see us as we see one another. How else could God look at a profane fisherman and see an evangelist? How could He look at Mary Magdalene and see a saint? How can He look at you and me and see anything worth saving? We will never be able to answer the "how" of that question. We only know that He did. He saw through the rough, repulsive exterior and loved us for what we could become through His grace. How else can I explain God's call to me?

Surely Heaven never looked down upon more unpromising human material than the sun-browned, barefoot boy who followed the plow through the North Carolina tobacco patch. The boy was just as stubborn and willful as the mule that pulled the plow. I know, because I was the boy, and from long association, summer after summer, I had come to know the mule even better than I understood myself. I was spoiled and selfish, and in all of my efforts to recall anything good or commendable about myself from those earliest years, I have always drawn a blank. It was not that I wanted to be wicked. I had every reason to believe that God had something special for me to do, but I did not know Jesus as a personal Friend until my early teens.

It was while I dug my toes into the cool fresh furrow of

the first spring plowing that God called me to make a decision which was to change my entire life. I can still relish the thrill of getting Dad's permission to go barefooted for the first time on that early spring morning. My brother Norman and I leaped for joy. Other memories are not so clear, but I can savor that particular scene to this very day—the birds swooping down behind me into the freshly turned furrow, the blue sky above, the glorious sense of freedom, and above all else the exultation of spirit. God spoke to me while I plowed and the greatest decision of my life was made when I completely turned the reins of my life over to Jesus Christ. I'm still amazed that He sought me out and called me to be a minister for Him. Oh, the wonders of redeeming love and grace!

From my earliest childhood memories about Mother, one recurring impression has always stood out: her telling and retelling about the polio which almost took my life and how God had saved me for a purpose.

It was known as infantile paralysis in the year 1928 when the disease zeroed in on Greensboro, North Carolina, to make that area the epidemic center of the world. Hundreds of children were stricken by it, and most of them were dying, because the medical profession knew absolutely no remedy that could counteract the crippling malady. I was three and a half years of age when the disease struck me and the doctors did not hold out any hopes at all for my recovery. The particular type of polio which I had contracted apparently affected the spine and brain, building up an intolerable pressure which finally depressed the vital actions of the brain. When the doctors tapped my spine to relieve the mounting pressure, the fluid shot almost to the ceiling. The prognosis was for more and more pressure until it would block the life-giving areas of the brain. A doctor was sent to the waiting room to inform my parents that there were no further grounds for hope, and that I could not live more than thirty minutes.

My dear Christian mother was the only one who would not accept that fatalistic report. She refused to believe that God was going to allow me to die. Her fervent prayers constantly ascended for my deliverance from death. Within an hour the physicians were astounded to learn that the spinal pressure was decreasing instead of following the normal course of increase! And after a ravaging attack on my right arm and shoulder, creating a permanent disability, the disease spent its fury.

Contrary to the "Kenny" treatments for polio which were later developed, the doctors ordered that both of my arms be completely immobilized by wooden braces, feeling that any muscle movement would be harmful. Of course that was exactly the opposite of what should have been done. Exercise and massage would have prevented much of the wasting which occurred in the inactive muscle. I can faintly recall the frustration of painful falls during that year, when I could not move an arm or a finger to protect myself from bumps and bruises.

Later, when Sister Kenny discovered the therapeutic value of water treatments and massage, my mother began a program of daily manipulation and massage of my arm and shoulder. No one will ever know how many hours she persisted in that exhausting routine of trying to rub life back into the wasted muscles of my right side. It was only in later years that I could appreciate the mother-love that went into those grueling treatments, treatments that probably saved my arm from being completely useless. As I became old enough to carry a load of farm work, my arm continued to gain in strength and facility. Although I still am not able to lift the right hand over my head, the exercises of plowing, forking hay, milking cows, etc., continued to supplement the persistent efforts of my mother's treatments, so that I have quite normal use of it in most activities today.

But Mother was not satisfied to depend on the physical therapy. She knelt with me to teach me the usual "Now I lay me down to sleep," but which always ended with the words, "And please help my arm to get better." For years, until I learned to talk to God as a personal Friend and Saviour, I prayed those words that Mother taught me, reflecting her faith and will that I should be completely restored.

2
Sixteen and Uncertain

Some of my fondest memories revolve around my years in the local public school. The school was adjacent to our farm and for eleven years I walked the quarter mile morning and night, and often at noontime as well. My classmates were close to me because we had studied together from the first grade right through the last year of high school.

My one great disappointment was being unable to excel in sports activities. The polio had affected me just enough to knock me out of any first-line participation. But even that proved to be a blessing in disguise. Time that might have been spent in empty exercise was directed more and more to the things of God. From my tobacco patch decision my experience with the Lord grew into a beautiful obsession.

I spent hours with my Bible and the sheer joy of knowing Christ and talking to Him much of every day, filled my life with constant delight. I remember kneeling one morning and making a covenant with the Lord to pray without ceasing. Having read the verse in the Bible, I felt that it must be possible to stay in an attitude of prayer all day long. On the way to school that morning, I talked to God as though He were walking physically by my side. I deliberately tried to keep a prayer in my heart every moment of that day, but alas, in the heat of the algebra class, my covenant slipped out of mind. I knew the first day had not been perfect but I was elated to think that most of the time I had been in heart communion with God.

The next day I remembered my decision and it was much easier to keep thoughts of God in my heart. I was so happy to find no one at home after school, because I could take my Bible to the barn haymow to study and pray. Day by day I learned one of the sweetest spiritual truths of the Bible by personal experience. I learned that it is possible to be in the spirit of prayer without ceasing. Later, in my hectic college years, that practice of the constant presence of God was to be my source of survival.

I also learned something else that was to be a reservoir of strength throughout my life and ministry. I discovered that people respect a person who is firm in his faith. My mother had lent me the characteristics of courage and persistence. Her own faith had been tested for years following her marriage, because my father was not a Christian. He had studied before they got married, had stopped using tobacco, and had even set the date for his baptism—immediately after the wedding. But he began to lose interest afterward, and it was not until his seventieth year that Dad finally followed through in giving his heart completely to Christ.

Mother's faith persisted and she taught us to pray for my father every day, even though it seemed so hopeless. But in my first year out of seminary, Dad came to Florida where I was interning as a young preacher, and asked to be baptized after the example of Jesus. That was one of the happiest experiences of my entire ministry, and for my dear mother it was the high point of her life. The last ten years of my father's life were undoubtedly the most satisfying of his full fourscore span of years.

Mother's faith had involved obedience to all of God's commandments. It was a robust religion that lived by action and not just a sentimental assent to truth. To her all the commandments were equally binding and to break one was to be guilty of sin. Since the fourth commandment clearly specified that "the seventh day is the sabbath of the LORD thy God; in it thou shalt not do any work," Mother passed along that seventh-day Sabbathkeeping as a part of her spiritual heritage to her children.

From the time she had discovered that fourth commandment in her Bible at the age of eighteen, Mother had boldly stepped out to start keeping the true Bible Sabbath. Just as soon as she had verified that the seventh day of the week was truly Saturday instead of Sunday (and she did this by consulting a variety of Protestant pastors), there was no hesitation in putting those convictions into action. She had a faith that required God to be first in her life, whether it was convenient or not. She was convinced by studying the Bible that the Sabbath should be observed from evening to evening, or sunset to sunset (Lev. 23:32; Mark 1:32). So each Friday was a beehive of activity in our big frame farmhouse. The old wood stove in the kitchen radiated aromas of cakes, pies and other baked delicacies.

My brother Norman and I had special duties also in getting ready for Sabbath. Water had to be drawn by windlass and rope from the deep sheltered well in the side yard. Bucket by bucket we carried it to the kitchen and poured it into the big water tank on the side of the stove. There it would warm during the day and be ready for the final ritual of bath taking just before sunset. That weekly scrubbing in the big tin washtub in the kitchen still lingers vividly in my mind.

At sundown, Norman and I would gather by Mother's chair and we would sing songs to welcome the blessed hours of the Sabbath. Dad would listen quietly from his big rocker. He never opposed our Christian beliefs and practices, and we did not try to pressure him into joining us. But after thirty years of observing Mother's Christ-like living, my father had to surrender. I'm convinced now that the consistent testimony of a godly life in the home is the most powerful evangelizing force in the world. It changed my father's life and it changed mine also. My mother's firm insistence upon putting Christ first, in spite of inconvenience, majority opinion, and even persecution, placed a mold on my life that has influenced it to this day.

At the little one-room clapboard church, just on the city limits of Kernersville, those convictions were reinforced through the years by Sabbath School teachers who patiently taught me to stand for principle though the heavens fall. Daniel and his friends in Babylonian captivity became my childhood heroes. They preferred to die in the fiery furnace than to yield up their faith. Joseph was another Bible character who influenced my life tremendously. I knew every detail of his experience as he suffered test after test in Egypt without compromising his faith. To this very day I find it difficult to read of his reconciliation with his brothers without weeping. Some of my most lasting decisions to be faithful unto death grew out of those humble little classes which often were conducted under the trees in the churchyard.

In high school I had to start drawing on some of the moral courage that Mother had taught us to exercise. It wasn't easy being a Sabbathkeeper in a public school. Many students had been molded by the prejudices of the parents and looked upon Saturday as "that old Jewish Sabbath." Actually, of course, the Sabbath was made and blessed by Christ Himself over two thousand years before the Jews came into existence, and nowhere is it spoken of in the Bible as Jewish. Luke, a Gentile writer, referred to many things that were especially Jewish, such as "the synagogue of the Jews" and the "Passover of the Jews," but never the "Sabbath of the Jews." The Bible speaks of the seventh day as "the Sabbath of the Lord," "Lord's Day," or "My holy day."

I soon found out, though, that my classmates actually respected my religious convictions. Many of them had sat by me from the first grade, and most of them knew of my teenage commitment to follow Christ fully. Knowing that I would not attend activities on Friday nights or Sabbath, they planned our class functions at other times. I was elected president of my Junior class, and was also an officer of the Senior class.

But as graduation day approached, a bitter disappointment loomed on the horizon. I discovered that the school administration had set the commencement exercises for Friday night and that the invitations had already been printed. Word immediately spread that I would not attend. Classmates talked to the principal, and the principal called me to his office. He apologized for making the mistake of scheduling the service for Friday night, but pleaded with me to make an exception for this special program. I explained my convictions and assured him that it was impossible for me to attend the graduation. Even though I deeply desired to graduate with the class I had known for eleven years, I still did not entertain the least serious thought of violating my conscience. At that time, my experience with Christ was so deep and wonderful that I never would have considered willfully breaking His commandment.

Other teachers were called in to use the persuasive influence, but to no avail. I felt sorry for Mr. Cude, the principal, because I knew he was genuinely sorry for the mistake and truly wanted me to be in the graduation. Finally he said, "Well, in order to get you to the program on Friday night, I must tell you that you have the Civitan Award." That was the first intimation that I had won the coveted scholarship awarded each year to the best all-around student by the International Civitan Club. Always the announcement was reserved for the Commencement night, and the surprised student was called to the front to be eulogized by the County Superintendent of Public Instruction. The honored student was selected by the vote of fellow students, plus two votes by each teacher.

Pleased though I was by the unexpected honor, I patiently explained to the perplexed principal why I could not, under any circumstances, attend the graduation on Friday night. Finally he said, "We'll just have to let the Superintendent explain why you are not present to accept the award." I heartily endorsed that suggestion. Later my friends told me about the reaction of hundreds who listened to the award presentation speech. The Superintendent said, "We do not condemn Joe because he is not here to receive this award. We are proud of him because he is not here. That is one of the reasons he is being honored tonight. He is true to his conscience and to principle. His Sabbath began at sundown tonight, and he would not violate his conscience to be here, as much as he wanted to graduate with his class." I'm sure he gave a much better speech about me because I was not present, than if I had been there in person.

When many of my worldly friends congratulated me, not for the award, but for not being at the meeting, I knew that my absence had made a greater impact than a thousand sermons. I secretly purposed in my heart never to let people or circumstances sway me from obeying the commandments of God.

The Civitan scholarship included a year's tuition at nearby Guilford College, a Quaker institution. I was only sixteen years of age and had no idea at all what I should prepare for as a life work. But since the college was only eight miles from my home, I decided to hitchhike back and forth each day and just take a regular freshman course of basic subjects. My faith was strong that God would lead me into a choice that could glorify Him.

All during that year I prayed for guidance in what I should study and, strange as it now seems, not once did the gospel ministry suggest itself to my thinking until Mrs. Mattie Lucas came to stay with us near the end of the school year. She was a dedicated Bible teacher who had joined an evangelistic crusade team in a nearby town. Never before or since have I met a person with a sweeter Christian bearing than Mrs. Lucas.

For two weeks she occupied our guest room, visiting families during the day, and in the evening, before and after the preaching service, quietly changing my life by a few well-chosen words. Although I've been tempted to think that Mother might have put her up to it, I now feel that it was the Holy Spirit who led her to question me as I walked into the house one evening. Abruptly she asked, "Joe, what are you studying to be in your college course?" I replied that I was just taking a general course inasmuch as I had not decided on a life vocation. Then, fixing her wonderful, expressive eyes upon me she said, "Joe, I believe God wants you to be a minister. I think you would make a tremendous worker for God."

Those were probably the most shocking words I had ever heard in my life. For some strange reason the thought of being a minister had never seriously entered my head. Oh, I had been impressed by some preachers all right. I marveled that men could stand up and speak with fluency and ease. Even though I could be very relaxed in groups and had the social graces to get on well with people, I was absolutely terrified of speaking to an audience. I don't remember how I parried the remark of our Bible teacher guest, but she made it a point to speak briefly again and again about her convictions during the next two weeks.

Certain it is that she never knew what a turmoil her words were causing in my heart. The Spirit who led her to say them would not allow me to forget them. I was awed by the thought that somebody believed I could be a minister. Day after day as the final semester passed, the thought grew into a decision. Prayers and tears sealed the growing conviction that God had a special work for me to do.

I talked to only one person about my agony of decision and that was Wilma Knight, a lovely girl with whom I had developed a special friendship at the college. Both of us sang in the a capella choir and during the spring New England choir tour we had discovered some unusual common spiritual interests. She was a dedicated Christian of the Friends persuasion, and constantly engaged me in debates on evolution and Bible doctrines. She also lived in the community and was a day student like myself, so we would eat our lunch together each day under the big campus trees. She was delighted to know that I was considering the ministry, and gave me every encouragement to obey the call of God. Before the school year ended I had made decisive plans to apply the next September to Southern Junior College near Chattanooga, Tennessee, to study for the ministry.

My last summer at home seemed to fly by, and final preparations were made for the long train trip to Collegedale, Tennessee. My next door girl cousin, Rachel, who was as close to me as a sister, was going to travel with me and enroll as a freshman at the college. Plans were laid for us to leave on Saturday night from the train station of the neighboring town of Kernersville.

On Friday afternoon I drove down to Guilford College for a final visit with Wilma. We spent the hours as usual, studying the Bible and singing some of the beautiful music we had learned together in the choir. She wanted me to practice a new duet arrangement of the prayer song, "Bless This House," and we sang it to the applause of her mother and little brother and sister. It was a pleasurable visit that I was to live over a thousand times in my mind.

Little did I sense the tragedy that was to unfold in that family within a few short hours.

I left reluctantly as the sun was lowering toward the horizon. It was not easy to drive out of the yard that day, but Wilma's picture was on the seat beside me, and we had agreed to keep in close touch by letter. The Sabbath came and passed. Our train pulled out of Kernersville station on Saturday night amid a few tears. Sunday passed by and Monday morning dawned. I was registering at Southern Junior College in Collegedale, Tennessee, but back in Guilford, Wilma was preparing to leave home to register for her second year at Guilford College. She was ironing a dress on the back porch about eight o'clock in the morning. A plane had just taken off from the nearby Tri-City Airport. As it struggled to gain altitude something happened and it began to nose downward. With a dying scream it crashed into the back porch of Wilma's home and exploded. She was killed, along with her mother, little brother, and little sister. Her grandmother leaped through a window to safety and another sister barely escaped the blazing inferno.

News reached me the next day, and I was stunned. Only three days earlier I had stood among those people singing, "Bless this house 0 Lord I pray, keep it safe by night and day." Now they were gone and the house was no more. I realized then that my Bible study was probably the last spiritual appeal they had heard. It was a crushing experience. For the first time I came face-to-face with the truth that my work would involve decisions of eternal life or death. Burning through my grief was the question as to whether I had said everything I should have said to prepare them for eternity. Many times in the intervening years I have given invitations to souls who would never live to hear another. But in only one or two instances did I recognize that I was presenting their last opportunity to be saved.

3
College Romance and Narrow Escape

The next four years of my life were surely the most exciting and fulfilling that I had ever experienced. For the first time I was associated with young people who shared my religious convictions and all my teachers were godly Christian counselors. The college was located in a beautiful valley amidst nature's most profuse demonstration of flower and fauna. To this day, I have not found a spot more calculated to inspire and uplift the soul.

Because my parents were able to provide only a token of the financial help I needed, I took advantage of the work opportunities on the campus. Along with a full load of heavy college subjects, I found myself committed to thirty hours a week painting broom handles at the college broom shop. This schedule meant going to work at six o'clock in the morning, working until noon, and then dashing to a full afternoon of classes. Study came only for two hours or so in the evening, lights went out at ten o'clock and the morning seemed to dawn almost immediately afterward. There seemed to be so little time for prayer and Bible study. Fortunate it was that I had learned to practice God's presence and to pray without ceasing. Much of my communion with God was done as I dipped broom handles and rushed from work to classes.

By the end of my second year the college had upgraded from a junior college to three college grades and the following year the fourth grade was added to make it a full-fledged senior college with a new name—Southern

Missionary College. It would be my honor to serve as president of the first graduating class from the newly accredited school.

Several events during those college years convinced me of two things. First, God was watching over me and guiding the course of my life. Second, Satan was very angry about my decision and was determined to destroy me if possible. At least three times during those four years my life was spared only by a direct miraculous intervention of God. Aside from those dramatic episodes, which I will share with you briefly, God demonstrated His grace to me in a hundred different providential ways which I will not have time to relate in this small book.

One of the greatest of those blessings came in a most unusual manner, and it had to do with a prayer which I had been offering almost daily since my decision to become a minister. Earnestly I had requested God to lead me to the girl who could share with me in the work of soul winning. I felt that God was preparing, somewhere, somebody that I had never met, perhaps in the same way He had been preparing me, and that in due time He would bring our paths together. Of one thing I was certain, the kind of wife I chose would be I the greatest factor in the kind of minister I would become. That was why it had become a subject of almost daily prayer from the time God had led me to accept His call.

God's answer, as I said, came in a very unusual way. Near the middle of the school year I was hurriedly shaving in the third floor washroom of the men's dormitory. Other boys were shaving at the long mirror on either side of me. Suddenly my private meditations were interrupted by the voice of one boy down the line who was enthusiastically talking to his friend. He was describing in the most extravagant language the attributes of a girl from his home town who was a freshman nursing student at the college. It was obvious that the young fellow was quite smitten by the girl, but it was also obvious that he had not made too much progress with her. But it was his description which fascinated me. If he was telling the truth, he was actually describing the girl I had determined to find and marry. It was all there in his glowing description—beauty, talent, spirituality, background and intelligence. I strained my ear to catch the name of the girl, and finally, almost casually, he let the name drop—Lu Ann. I repeated it over to myself several times so that I would not forget until there was a chance to look it up in the directory of students.

Later, as I scanned the list of students by their first names, I was relieved to find that there was only one girl with the name of Lu Ann—Lu Ann Tunison. I had never heard the name before and had no idea what she looked like. But it didn't take long, later that day, to make a few discreet inquiries in the cafeteria, and by evening chapel worship I knew exactly what Lu Ann Tunison looked like. It was apparent that the boy had been right in the physical assessment, but I was much more concerned about the spiritual qualities. From past experience in secular schools I had been completely turned off by the shallow, superficiality of many attractive girls. So I determined to find an occasion to meet her personally.

The next morning at early breakfast I was assigned by the dining hall hostess to a table with several other young people. After some casual chatter, the students finished their breakfast one by one and excused themselves until finally only one girl remained with me at the table. Suddenly it dawned on me that she might be acquainted with Lu Ann Tunison, so I gathered the courage to ask if she were. Suddenly the girl came alive. Of course she knew Lu Ann—she was Harriet, her roommate! And for the next fifteen minutes I listened in astonishment to the same kind of incredible eulogy that the young man had delivered while he was shaving. Except Harriet added much more about the tremendous spiritual depth, the love of prayer and Bible study, and the fascination with nature. It seemed too good to be true. I had never met a girl in all my life who matched the description that those two people had given me.

Needless to say, my interest was now raised to a new high point. At noontime I waited to join the cafeteria line until Lu Ann had taken her tray on the opposite side, then I carefully timed myself to leave the line when she did, placing us at the same table. From that day I was convinced that her friends had told me only truth about her remarkable qualities.

Over the next two years our friendship slowly matured. There were manifold indications that God was directing in a most positive way. Later I learned that she had been praying for God to lead the life of the unknown young man who would someday ask for her hand in marriage.

At the end of the second college year Lu Ann had to leave the beautiful Collegedale valley and continue her next three years of nursing in Washington D.C. It was a painful experience for both of us. Washington was over 600 miles away. On the final day together we hiked to the top of old Grindstone Mountain on the opposite side of the valley, and there I asked her to be my wife. She accepted, and we knelt together as we had done so often before, to commit our lives completely into God's hands for service. It was a day neither of us would ever forget. We descended the winding trail and later that same evening she boarded the train that was to separate us for the next two years.

The following year was the most crucial of my college career. Satan focused a barrage of attacks against my spiritual commitment, and actually tried to take my life on three separate occasions. One of those brushes with death took place on a crowded Trailways bus. Our a capella choir had spent an enjoyable weekend giving concerts in Atlanta, Georgia. The final program had been presented under the inspired direction of our beloved "Fessor" Dortch. It was almost midnight and the bus had just passed the halfway point on the way back to Collegedale. Fifty tired and sleepy student singers had finally settled down to fitful slumber in their comfortable seats. All of them, that is, except one. Maurice Abbott on the bumpy back seat found it difficult to relax. So, just as the bus pulled into the city limits of Ringgold, Maurice stood in the aisle, stretched, and made his way slowly to the front. Standing near the front seat he watched sleepily as the driver steered expertly past the last of the city street lights.

To Maurice it was a familiar route; he had hitchhiked through the town often on his weekend leaves. In a moment the road would divide, and the Collegedale Pike would angle off to the left. But as the driver approached the wide division in the highway, unfamiliar with his special run, he aimed the big bus toward the right hand lane. Instantly, Maurice was wide awake. "No," he said excitedly, "It's the left fork to Collegedale." The driver applied the brakes and turned sharply to the left, the wide open angle of the fork still allowing him space and time to swing into the proper approach.

Just as the bus completed its sudden, lumbering 90-degree turn to the left, the air was filled with the deafening roar of a speeding train which flashed by the right side of the bus. The driver braked to a halt and, jolted awake, I sat paralyzed as the locomotive screamed past, seemingly only inches from the bus window from which I watched in fascinated horror. Long after the vibrating noise had faded into the distance, a dead silence still gripped the passengers. Finally a small voice asked, "Driver, did you see the train?" He answered quickly, "No, I didn't even know the railroad was there."

There was no doubt about what had happened. Our bus had been headed straight across the tracks. If Maurice had not corrected the driver at the last split second, barely in time for the driver to swing left, parallel to the tracks, all of us would probably have been dead. There would have been no way for the train to avoid striking the bus exactly in the middle, had we proceeded on in the right fork. And I noted with a shudder that I was sitting with my cousin Rachel in the exact middle seat of the right section of the bus. Now I had another strong reason to believe that God had some special work for me to do for Him.

How often it seems that the turn of a very insignificant event can affect the destinies of a multitude. In this case, fifty lives were spared by a simple act of impulse on the part of one student. But who can believe that it was only coincidental when that casual act occurred at the one precise moment when it could save half a hundred young people from death? It certainly was an unrehearsed and spontaneous incident from the human viewpoint, but in the providence of God it was anything but accidental. Angels overruled in the meshing of those circumstances. Someday I want to talk to those angels and understand more clearly how God frustrated the devil's clever plot to destroy that busload of singers.

4
Angel in My Tent

Following that hectic third year of college, I entered the most traumatic summer of my life. As a change from two previous summers of religious book sales work, I made arrangements to work with an experienced evangelist in Valdosta, Georgia. Living in a small tent behind the crusade big top, I led the singing each evening, did some evangelistic visiting, and kept the tent chairs and equipment in order. It was a wonderful experience for a young aspiring minister, and in spite of poor attendance, I was excited about that first taste of actual face-to-face soulwinning. Another anticipated delight later in the summer was Lu Ann's two-week vacation, after the first year of nurses' training. Our plans by mail included my spending a weekend at her home in Pensacola, Florida, if it could be coordinated with the evangelistic crusade.

Then it happened. Just a week before her vacation began I awoke one morning with chills, fever, and a special concentration of pain in my neck and spine. All day I stayed in bed, dosing myself with the usual run of "bug" remedies, but with little noticeable effects. By evening it was obvious that I was not able to lead the song service. A young medic soldier by the name of Eddie from nearby Moody Field volunteered to take my place on the platform that night, and afterward he and his buddy came back to my little tent to see how I was doing. Their limited exposure to medical symptoms convinced them that I was suffering an attack of malaria, a rather common occurrence in the south Georgia area. They insisted on bundling me into the car for a midnight drive to the medical laboratory on the military base where they worked. By a simple blood smear they would be able to determine if I had malaria. Feverish, and with no other assistance in sight, I accepted their offer.

It was very late into the night when the tests were completed, and all malaria blood smears showed no signs of such an infection at all. Relieved at least over the negative results of the lab tests, we were crossing the parking lot to get into the car when the medical doctor of the base drove in beside us. The boys introduced me to the officer and explained briefly to him what they had been doing in the lab. It was an incidental encounter and a moment later we were driving towards the exit gate of the facility.

Suddenly we heard a faint shout and looked back quickly to see the medical officer waving for us to stop. Eddie braked and backed up to where the doctor was standing by the back hospital entrance. "Bring him in and let me take a look at your patient," he said to my uniformed friends. Surprised that he had given us a second thought, we followed him into the examining room. Within minutes he had me on the table, probing and thumping in the mysterious ways of doctors. Suddenly his head jerked up, he yanked off his glasses and looked at me in disbelief. "You have meningococcemia."

The word didn't make sense to me, but I could tell from the serious expression on the doctor's face that it must be as bad as it sounded. Swiftly he poured pills into his hand and began to pass them to the two medics with terse instructions to swallow them immediately. Then it was pills for me, and a massive injection, while he explained the nature of my illness. I had meningitis which was still only in the blood stream, but which could reach the spinal column at any moment. The prognosis after that was for agonizing death within an hour or two.

Everyone I had been in contact with for days would have to take preventive medication.

I was rushed to the hospital isolation unit to spend the next week receiving intensive antibiotic therapy. The following morning a painful spinal puncture was performed to see if the disease had penetrated the fluid. Fortunately it had not, and after seven days under hospital quarantine I was declared free of the disease in my blood.

Over and over as I lay on my back recovering from the spinal tap, I reviewed the chain of events which had brought me there. The sequence in the parking lot at midnight was the most incredible of all. Why had a military doctor driven into the parking lot precisely in time to meet us as we were leaving? What had caused him suddenly to call after us, when he had been so nonchalant and disinterested before? There was no doubt whatsoever that his last-second impulse to stop our car had saved my life. I would have dismissed my I chills and fever as a small indisposition that would spend its strength in a day or two. Alone in my little canvas room waiting for life and strength to return, I would probably have died within twenty-four hours.

I recalled the drama of the choir tour just weeks earlier. My life had been saved by the capricious mood of a boy who stood up to stretch and yawn on a bus. Now I had been saved by a voice that somehow called out in the fraction of time it could still be heard over the accelerating motor of Eddie's car. What if the student had not moved to the front of the bus? Suppose the doctor had been too preoccupied to worry over a small fever? And what if the wind had carried his voice the other way, or the noise of the motor had drowned out his shout? My very life had hinged upon some tiny casual actions that could just as well have never taken place. The more I thought of it, the more amazed I became, and the more convinced I was that none of those little circumstances had "just happened." I wanted to jump up from my bed and rush out of the isolation ward shouting out the news to everyone that God still works miracles.

Lu Ann's vacation coincided with my dismissal from the hospital, and she changed her train schedule to stop in Valdosta. Her mother had invited me to spend a few days in Pensacola, regaining my strength from the crisis, and Lu Ann,bless her heart, would travel with me the rest of the way. Since the Valdosta meetings were already drawing to a close, it was arranged that I would proceed to Chattanooga, Tennessee, to join another evangelistic series as soon as my strength permitted.

Those wonderful days at the water-front home of Lu Ann's parents were almost like a dream, and they passed all too quickly. From the screened porch we could watch the moon rise over the restless water of Pensacola Bay. We talked of our future, and especially about the plans we had laid for going to India as missionaries. A year before we had both made application to the Mission Board, and had circled India as the preferred field of labor. At Collegedale we had sat under the influence of a godly Bible teacher who had been a missionary in India for many years. Frank Ashlock's love for souls was contagious and we soon began to share the enthusiasm and excitement of working for the people he knew so intimately. Little did we realize then that we would some day actually be associated with Frank Marcella Ashlock in several years of mission service in the land of the maharajas. But in Pensacola in 1945 that experience existed only in the dreams that Lu Ann and I shared in whispers as we watched the moon rise higher over the bay.

Within a week I had to admit, even to myself, that my strength was fully restored, and Evangelist Stanley Harris was already launching his city-wide crusade in

Chattanooga, Tennessee. So I regretfully bade goodbye to my sweetheart and hurried northward to meet another amazing providence of God. Again I was slated to live in a small tent and lead the congregational singing each night. The huge canvas cathedral was located on McCallie Avenue, one of the main thoroughfares of the city. Hundreds crowded the tent every night in total contrast to the meager interest we had found in Valdosta. For the first time I had the thrill of actually visiting homes and helping people make their decisions for Christ. I tasted the intoxicating joys of soulwinning, and I knew from that time onward that I could never be satisfied doing anything other than public evangelism.

Near the end of the series I had such a terrifying encounter with the devil that I have shared it with only a few people in my whole life. For years only one other person knew of the experience, and that was Bob Wood, a close college friend who happened to stop by the tent to see me the very next morning after it happened. The evangelist had presented the subject of spiritualism the night before, and my visiting that day had almost wholly been given to exposing the devil's subterfuge and deception. I had heard that Satan always reacted angrily to this particular topic, but I had no idea that it would be so spectacular.

After fitfully sleeping until four o'clock in the morning, I was suddenly and violently awakened by hands around my throat that slowly tightened as I struggled to get free. Street lights cast an eerie glow through the canvas walls and every object in the tent was dimly visible. AND THERE WAS NO ONE IN THE TENT WITH ME! I was wide awake and the walls of the tent were lit up faintly by the outside lights. I tried to scream for help, but the pressure on my throat had cut off all sound. At the same time a horrible sense of fear swept over me. The very room seemed to be filled with the uncanny, skin-prickling presence of evil. In the midst of my thrashing about to escape the strangle-grip on my throat, words of prayer flashed through my mind. There was no time to consciously pray sentences, but the name of Jesus sought utterance through my lips. Then slowly the pressure began to relax around my neck, and in a moment it was gone completely.

The awful sense of evil remained, and I forced myself to drop off my cot to my knees to pray. I had to restrain myself from rushing out of the tent. It took all the strength of will I could muster to close my eyes and ignore the overwhelming terror welling up inside me. But gradually the panic subsided and my faith strengthened. Prayer brought peace to my heart, and glorious assurance. I crawled back into bed rejoicing and praising God for giving deliverance in the night

The next morning my friend Bob Wood came by the tent and I gave him the account of what happened. It was then that he pointed out the marks on my throat which I had not been able to see—marks which fully assured me that I had not been dreaming. The devil had made his third attack on my life within the period of one year, but God's power had prevailed once more. It was with those precious evidences of divine direction that I entered the last year of my education at Southern Missionary College.

5 Calamities and Comedies

That year of study was a strange mixture of bitter-sweet for me. It was very hard to be separated from the girl of my dreams, and yet there was a sense of excitement in being the president of the very first graduating class of a new senior college.

Some of the most pleasant memories of that year revolve around the activities of our male quartet, the Heralds of Prophecy. It was my special joy to be a part of that official college quartet for four years, and sometimes I think how easy it would be to write another book about our adventures in representing the school all over the Southland.

Max Ritchie was not only the second tenor in the quartet, but he had been my canvassing partner for a summer of colporteur work in Hillsboro, North Carolina. We were as close as any blood brothers could be, and that friendship has continued through the years.

I sang second bass, and the baritone was carried by Jim Evans who was also my dormitory roommate for one year. The fourth member of the group was Jack Just, who had the sweetest tenor voice on the campus.

What a bond grew between us as we traveled and put on student recruitment concerts for the college!

Even though forty years have passed by, I can still recall some of the memorable experiences—some humorous and heartwarming—which marked our camaraderie and fellowship. Of course, some were not so pleasant either.

Once we were asked to sing for a funeral in nearby Chattanooga. A poor man had been blown to bits in a terrible explosion at the Hercules Powder Company. We had been asked to sing a family favorite for the funeral which was held in a little mountain church house. This time the note was softly sounded by one of the quartet on a pitch pipe. But, unfortunately, it wasn't quite loud enough for everybody to hear it. The one who blew the note assumed that all of us had it, so he boldly began singing. Too late, we found that each man had started in a different key, and it was impossible to stop. We struggled manfully through all three stanzas in what must have been one of the most agonizing, discordant musical messages ever delivered for the purpose of comforting anybody. I can only believe that we added to everybody's distress that day. Incredibly, all four of us were convinced that we could find the right note and quickly correct our opening mistake. When we couldn't manage it, we were too embarrassed to stop and start over!

Near the end of the school year our quartet was invited to sing for a Sunday night evangelistic meeting in Lenoir City, Tennessee, which was about 80 miles from the college. Jim drove us there in his beat-up Ford, but all of us together could not scrounge up enough money to buy gas for the round trip. We figured that the evangelist or the church would take care of the cost, so we barely scraped together sufficient money for a one-way trip.

We took another student, Charles Witt, to play the piano for the song service. Jim led the music and introduced our twenty-minute program to a very appreciative audience. Afterward, to our dismay, no one offered to reimburse us or meet any of the expenses involved. It was ten o'clock at I night and five penniless students had empty stomachs and an empty gas tank.

We got our heads together and concluded that it was

impossible to get back to the college without a refill of both fuel and food. Just across the street from the evangelistic tent was a brightly lit all-night restaurant. All the church crowd had departed from the tent, but the eating place seemed well attended still, by the cars all around it.

We tuned up near the front door and began to harmonize. Everybody within hearing distance started drifting in our direction. By the end of the second stanza of "I've Been Working on the Railroad" we had a sizable audience. After four or five songs we were literally surrounded by the most responsive crowd we had ever seen.

We kept nudging each other because we knew somebody had to take up an offering. Finally, Max gathered the courage to make a little speech and told them that Charles would pass his hat for a little love offering.

To our delight the money began to pour into that old hat. Later we moved inside the restaurant and got permission to sing for the patrons. Again the hat was passed up and down the counter, and the applauding customers emptied their pockets of change.

When the impromptu concert was over, we counted our treasure at a corner table and found we had enough for a satisfying meal, a fill up of Jim's car, and about two dollars! each beyond all the expenses.

In those days very few students were able to afford an automobile. This created a real transportation problem for me, because I had determined to make that trip up Highway 11 at least twice a year to see my beloved Lu Ann.

My usual mode of travel was "by thumb," and I had developed a degree of expertise in hitchhiking from Tennessee to Washington, D.C.

My friend, Bob Wood, also had a girlfriend who was taking nurses' training with Lu Ann, so we made plans to go there together during the 1945 Christmas holidays. The first lap of our journey was across the Smoky Mountains by bus for a short visit with my parents in North Carolina. From there our plan was to hitchhike into Greensboro and then on up Highway 29 into Washington, D.C.

My folks lived in a large farmhouse beside the main highway linking Winston-Salem and Greensboro. We chose to leave on a bitterly cold day, and it was hard to walk away from the warmth of the big wood stove into the icy blast of wind. Nevertheless, we carried our heavy suitcases out to the roadside and put on our most appealing smiles as we extended our thumbs.

After fifteen minutes I was quite numb with the cold and suggested that we run back in the house to thaw out. Bob said, "You go ahead. I'll keep your suitcase, and if I get a ride, I'll meet you at the bus station in Greensboro." From the living room window I had a clear view of the road. My body was just beginning to respond to the radiant heat of the stove when I heard the sound of a car stopping. Glancing out I saw Bob hauling our two suitcases into the back of an ancient, open-bed pickup truck.

Five minutes after it had driven away, I was ready to face the cold again. Feeling a bit disappointed that I had missed the ride with Bob, I hopefully watched the next car approach. It was a brand new Lincoln, and it pulled to a stop directly in front of me. A friendly young man asked me where I was headed, and I told him I needed to get to the bus station. He replied, "You're in luck. I'll be going right by the station."

A few miles down the road we whizzed past the old truck. Bob was huddled in the back holding his ears against the freezing wind. I rolled down the window and waved to him as we passed. He looked anything but happy.

Ten miles later the driver dropped me in front of the bus depot, and I stepped inside just in time to encounter a classmate from my high school days. And I was talking to that pretty girl an hour later when Bob came stumbling in with the two suitcases, having walked about a mile from where he had been let out of the pickup. He was outraged and frozen as you can imagine.

My perverse sense of humor that day was to rebound upon me as the journey neared its end, and Bob would have the last laugh. By the time we had hop-scotched up the scenic Shenandoah Valley highway with half a dozen different cars and drivers I had become distinctly and painfully aware of a real physical problem. A fast-festering boil had developed in the very place where I could least afford to have it, and by the time we walked into Washington Sanitarium and Hospital, I was in constant agony. I also was unable to sit down, even in the most comfortable chair.

We went straight to the emergency room, because I knew that boil had to be treated before I would be able to visit my sweetheart. I had the feeling that Bob was not sensing the seriousness of my situation as he should have.

The doctor also dealt with my crisis as though it was almost routine. He ordered me to undress and lie face down on the examination table. Then with an assisting nurse by his side he administered a localized injection to the site before lancing the boil to release the infection.

I felt an almost immediate relief, and pulled the sheet back over me as the doctor took care of his instruments. It was only then that I took notice of the attractive young nurse who had held the scalpel and assisted in the procedure. She was one of Lu Ann's best friends with whom we had often double-dated! She was averting her face as much as possible to save me embarrassment as well as herself.

When I rejoined Bob in the waiting room and explained who had assisted in my treatment, he no longer could restrain his laughter. It was obvious to me that he felt fully repaid for his frosty ride in the old pickup truck.

That senior year passed quickly. Almost every weekend was filled with student pastor duties in the small churches ringing the Collegedale valley. There I learned to think on my feet, and under the tutelage of dedicated Bible professors, learned to draw upon the exhaustless resources of God.

During that year I also came in contact with a statement which has continued to influence my preaching to this day. As I recall, it was shared with me by Professor Ludgate, who was the Greek and homiletics teacher. Later, as a parent and pastor I would read the statement repeatedly to draw strength for holding lines of principle in dealing with home and church problems. Nothing I ever learned in college or seminary did more to mold my life as a father and minister. Here's the statement:

> Those who have too little courage to reprove wrong, or who through indolence or lack of interest make no earnest effort to purify the family or the church of God, are held accountable for the evil that may result from their neglect of duty. We are just as responsible for evils that we might have checked in others by exercise of parental or pastoral authority, as if the acts had been our own.
>
> —*Patriarchs and Prophets*, p. 578.

That paragraph from a truly inspired book has given me the courage to draw lines and take positions even in the face of ridicule. I was convinced long ago that the truth will never be popular. Neither the world nor nominal Christians will applaud you for holding firmly to the right. It will often be necessary to stand alone in defense of convictions. The principle of standing for truth though the heavens fall was placed in my life by a saintly mother and godly Sabbath School teachers. And by the grace of God, I determined to be faithful to that principle until Jesus comes.

It was difficult to even imagine myself separating from the peaceful Collegedale valley where so much had happened to influence my life. But the school year literally flew by and our famous little class filed by to receive the first Southern Missionary College degrees from the hand of President Kenneth A. Wright. The last weeks of school had been marked by some difficult decisions. I had received more than one invitation to enter the pastoral ministry, but my mind was in a quandary about what to do. Lu Ann still had one year of nurses' training, and without a wife, I wondered just how effective I could be as a preacher. Student nurses were not even permitted to marry during their training period and that last year looked longer to me than the past three years combined.

Lu Ann was fighting a similar battle. The nurses' course was rigorous and discouraging, and she knew that I was chafing to get into the work of soulwinning. We had been engaged for two years already, and to wait for another year seemed unfair in the extreme. Both of us were temporizing about the possibility of her dropping out of nursing, although we dared not say too much about it to each other.

I sought counsel from my trusted friend and teacher, Frank Ashlock. He was sympathetic and took the time to tell me about the same decision he had faced as a young man. His nurse wife-to-be had a year of training left when he finished college also, and they had waited for her to finish. Later, as missionaries, they had been grateful that she had completed the course which enriched their foreign service. He advised me to wait and let Lu Ann graduate from nursing. I could see the wisdom and reason behind his counsel but my heart was talking louder than my head right at the moment. I didn't want to wait another year.

Finally, after much prayer and heart searching, I told the Lord that He would have to give me the answer. I was willing to do whatever He asked me to do, but to please let me know for sure which way to go. In my prayer I asked God to reveal His will beyond the shadow of a doubt. As I closed my prayer, I reached out to the Bible before me and opened it entirely at random. Then looking down at the first text which caught my eye on the open page, I read these words, "Wait on the LORD: be of good courage, and he shall strengthen thine heart: wait, I say, on the LORD" (Ps. 27:14). With a sigh of relief I closed the Bible and bowed my head in thanksgiving that the question was now sealed and settled. It had happened in a moment of time, but I had no doubt that God had revealed His will to me from His Word.

In the far future I often would look back to that decision as one of the wisest choices I could have made. Like my mentor Frank Ashlock, I found that the challenges of medical needs in India made Lu Ann's nursing experience a tremendous advantage. And later still, when our youngest son passed through the terminal weeks of a malignant brain tumor, it was Lu Ann's skill in nursing which enabled us to care for him at home until he slipped into a final coma. How many times we thanked God for making that decision for us when our emotions might have led us to decide wrongly. Repeatedly we were shown the wisdom of waiting on the Lord and choosing the way of principle even though it involved temporary sacrifice and suffering. The test of true loyalty is in doing right because it is right in spite of emotional feelings or circumstances. The matter of standing for right though the heavens fall had proven once again to be a good rule of life.

6
A Tithing Miracle

With that matter settled it did not take long to make other related decisions. Conveniently, the Adventist Seminary was located within a few blocks of the hospital where Lu Ann was in training in Washington, D.C. Although I was tired of classes and longed to put my book learning into practice, I was also tired of being separated from the girl I loved. As soon as the graduation weekend was over I wrote a letter requesting an application for enrollment in the fall semester of the seminary, with a candidacy for Master of Arts degree in Systematic Theology.

Then I began to look around for a summer job to help meet the heavy expense of room and board in a big city like Washington. After some deliberation, I decided that colporteur book sales would provide the best opportunity to win souls and help fit me for the work of evangelism as well.

It was a pleasant surprise when settling my financial account at the college, to learn that I had a credit of $132. The year was 1946 and $132 was just exactly enough money to buy an ancient Model A Ford that I desperately needed for my summer sales work. I had already seen it advertised, and with money in hand, I was preparing to close the deal. But before I could actually finish the transaction, a sudden disconcerting thought flashed through my mind. In retrospect, I'm sure that thought was sent from God. I remembered that for all five years of college life, due to my polio disability, small monthly checks had been credited to my account from the State

Vocational Rehabilitation. Since the money never passed through my hands, I had almost forgotten about the allowance. But now I was struck by the thought that no tithe had been paid on a cent of that money. I had scrupulously kept a record and tithed my college earnings, but not once had I remembered to tithe the credited amount from the state.

In dismay, I sat down to figure the total amount of aid over the five-year period. My feelings were mixed. I was grateful to discover the error in time to correct it, and yet I feared the possibility of having to borrow money to pay it. Finally the monthly figures were all collected and the columns added. I looked in disbelief at the total—$1320. I owed $132 tithe and that was the exact amount of my credit balance which *almost* had been spent on that Model A Ford.

I talked to some of my friends about the amazing coincidence of the amounts, and some of them strongly urged me to use the money for a car. "After all," they said, "You actually didn't get the money; it went to the school and you didn't spend it." They meant well, but I knew that the money was mine. It had paid tuition which I would have had to pay. With a sense of relief and inner peace I sealed the tithe envelope and dropped it into the offering plate the next Sabbath. I had no doubt about it being the right thing to do. There was no doubt in my mind either about the results of being faithful. I had seen miracles in my own family as a result of giving the tenth to God. Had not God said "Bring ye all the tithes into the storehouse that there may be meat in mine house, and prove me now herewith, saith the LORD of hosts, if I will not open you the windows of heaven, and pour you out a blessing that there shall not be room enough to receive it. And I will rebuke the devourer for your sakes, and he shall not destroy the fruits of your ground" (Mal. 3:10, 11).

Later at the end of the summer, I would have reason to believe that promise more than ever. In response to my faith, God worked a miracle that restored to me almost three times the amount I had dropped into the tithe plate. And even though I had to walk miles on foot between the country homes, I would not exchange the experience of that summer for two deluxe model A Fords. I think you will agree when I share that experience with you.

The assigned territory where I was to sell religious books centered in Lake City, South Carolina. It was a big tobacco selling town, and also claimed to have the biggest bean market in the world. My partner, Walter Ralls, had arrived ahead of me only to find every available room rented to the tobacco buyers. After a house-to-house inquiry, he had managed to rent a room in a private home. When I arrived the problem was even more acute, so I started canvassing the homes for a room also. Finally a young contractor had pity on me and agreed to rent the guest room that was seldom occupied in his home. That's how I became a part of the Askins family for the summer of 1946. Bill and his wife had three lovely children and I soon was made to feel just like a member of the household.

On the first Sunday with the Askins, Bill asked me to go to church with him. He was a member of the Men's Bible Class at the First Baptist Church, and I soon discovered that almost all the business and professional people in town were members of that same class. Since there was no Sabbathkeeping church in the city, I accepted the invitation. The class was tremendously warm and friendly and Bill introduced me to many of the hundred men who crowded the downstairs facility.

The pastor was the regular teacher of the group, but he had just accepted a call to another congregation. The president of the class, the city attorney, taught the lesson that Sunday. It was obviously a bit out of his line and he closed the discussion by asking various members to teach the lesson the following Sunday. One after another the men declined, and finally in apparent desperation, he asked me if I would take the class the next week. When I accepted, an audible sigh of relief went up from the group.

No one had yet learned that I was a young preacher in training. As far as they were concerned I was just a friend of Bill's and they were all relieved that they would not be asked to teach. After the dismissal, the lawyer gave me a copy of the adult quarterly with the new series of lessons beginning the following Sunday.

Later that day I had a chance to look over the quarterly, and imagine my surprise to find that the entire series was on the ten commandments The first two lessons dealt with the relationship of law and grace, and each of the remaining lessons focused on one of the commandments. I was delighted to read strong statements in the lesson notes upholding the great moral law as the standard of the judgment. The lesson for July 14, 1946, had this tremendous comment:

> "The ten commandments incorporate in a wonderful way the moral law of God. They present in practical terms the demands of God upon man's conduct. The moral laws of God are as binding on our conduct and destiny as are the laws of nature. No man can violate them with impunity. ... Anyone who thinks himself to be exempt from the moral law of God revealed in the ten commandments is mistaken."

God blessed in the preparation of the lesson, and never have I felt greater freedom in speaking to a group. The men sat as though entranced by the topic of the law in relation to grace and faith. After the class they asked me to be their regular teacher, and I accepted. That was the beginning of a wonderful three months' association with an unusual group of Baptist men whose friendship I cherish to this day. The mayor, the doctors, and the business leaders of the city became first-name friends with whom I maintained contact for years. Week by week I led the group in thrilling Bible studies about obedience and the joys of full commitment to Christ.

A special committee approached me in the middle of the summer begging me to consider a call that might be extended to become the pastor of the church. A new visiting minister spoke each Sunday on a trial basis, but none had satisfied the pulpit committee. Usually, the guest minister sat in my class during the lesson time, leaving a few minutes early to prepare for the worship service.

Honored though I was as a very young and inexperienced preacher, I assured the committee that I was committed to a Sabbathkeeping faith and that my goal was to be a foreign missionary in the near future. Although the Bible Class had known nothing of my religious beliefs when they first invited me to teach, they quickly learned that it involved obedience to all of God's Word. Over and over they expressed appreciation for that particular facet of my faith. Almost every Sunday I was invited home for lunch by one of the class, and many extra hours of Bible study resulted. It was my joy to lead one member to a decision for Christ, and nineteen years later I found him still faithful to his Christian commitment.

The final week of my stay was especially busy because I had to deliver hundreds of books which had been ordered during the summer. Nevertheless, I felt obligated to the members of my Bible Class who had arranged extra speaking appointments so that their wives could hear me before I left. Besides the Wednesday night prayer meeting for the whole church, I spoke to the B.T.U. officers on

Tuesday night, and all Sunday School officers and teachers on Thursday night. Then I taught my last lesson to a packed class of over a hundred on Sunday morning. At the end of the class, Rack Whitlock, the city attorney, made a speech expressing appreciation and handed me an envelope. It contained a letter signed by the class members and a check signed by the class treasurer. The letter assured me that I would be getting a monthly check from the class during the next year to help meet my seminary expenses. And for the next thirteen months, while I studied at the Adventist seminary, that Baptist check arrived to make up almost exactly what I needed for meeting the expenses of the year. In fact, when I got married the week after graduating, I had the sum total of $20 with which to launch the next exciting phase of my life—this time with the lovely girl for whom I had waited impatiently for three years.

I must not forget to tell you that the amount received from the Men's Bible class totaled almost three times the amount of the $132 which I had sealed into the tithe envelope at the beginning of the summer. I certainly did not anticipate that God would honor His promise in such an unusual way. That is probably the first time in history that a Southern Baptist church helped pay the expenses of a Sabbathkeeping minister in the Seventh-day Adventist Seminary. I believe I would have missed the joy of that experience had I not been faithful in returning the tithe to God in full measure.

7
Double Trouble at the Bus Stop

Lu Ann graduated as a registered nurse during the same week that I received my Master of Arts degree in systematic theology. Our wedding was scheduled for October 5 immediately following our graduations. As you can imagine, it was a most exciting occasion. For many weeks I had been marking off the days on the seminary library wall calendar. The girls at the desk indulged my daily ritual of X-ing out the current date and leafing through the remaining days before October 5. I was one of only two unmarried students in the seminary family and most of the faculty and students knew about my approaching marriage. Dr. Roland Loasby, my Greek professor, was to honor the occasion by performing the rites in the seminary chapel.

A month before graduation, through the good graces of my father's co-signature, I entered the ranks of mature manhood by purchasing my first automobile—on credit, of course. Since cars had not been manufactured during the war years, I had no alternative but to reach back past 1943 to acquire the latest model—already six years of age. And the cost was highly inflated, even for that vintage. I was fortunate to find an exceptional, clean 1941 Ford club coupe, which served well for the first two well-traveled years of our married life.

It was that shiny, maroon Ford which almost turned my wedding day into a nightmare. I still have a hard time believing the crazy chain of events which created the problem. Two weeks before the wedding, while driving past the Washington Sanitarium bus stop, I noticed a lady run down the hill, only to miss the departing bus by seconds. She looked vaguely familiar, and anyway, it was customary to pick up people at the bus stop because they were almost always employees or visitors at the Sanitarium where Lu Ann had taken her training. They had to ride the bus a mile to the transfer station just by the seminary, and then transfer to any part of Washington. The lady gratefully accepted my offer of a ride. It turned out that she had heard me sing at the weekly Sabbath vespers, and introduced herself as the sister of a well-known church worker in the area. She was fortyish and did sales work for a local institution. Five minutes of casual conversation and we were at the bus terminal where she graciously thanked me and joined the group of others who were bus-waiting.

I forgot the incident, as well as the lady's name; but a few days later—on October 5, to be exact—the incident suddenly grew into an emotional tempest—for me, that is. It was my wedding day, and I was up early in my apartment preparing to drive over to the seminary, when my landlady called me from downstairs. She said there was a letter for me. I hurried down to get it, quite curious because all of my friends and family knew I was leaving that address on October 5 and no more mail was expected. The envelope was not postmarked, but it was well sealed and clearly addressed to me. I opened it and read in amazement the unfamiliar handwriting of the most torrid love letter I had ever received in my life. It was so incredible that I quickly turned it over to the signature and there it was, the name of the lady I had picked up at the bus stop. At first I wanted to laugh at the utter stupidity of the whole thing; in fact, I think I did laugh, and asked the landlady if she knew the woman who had brought it to her door. She said, "Yes, it was poor Miss Blank. She does some very strange things, and doesn't seem to be all there." Well, I could buy that!

A few minutes later Earl Zager came in, the landlady's son and a close friend of mine. I told him about the funny letter, and he said, "Oh, that reminds me. Yesterday when you and Lu Ann were walking across the campus, Miss Blank asked me if you were going to marry that girl. When I said 'Yes,' she said emphatically, 'He can't do that, he is supposed to marry me.'" Suddenly the pit of my stomach got very weak, and the humor of the situation turned into stark fear. The wedding was only hours away. The woman would probably be there. The minister would ask the question, "If anyone knows any reason why this man and this woman should not be joined together in holy matrimony, let him now speak." Of course, Miss Blank would speak! She was obviously a mental case and she might do anything. Why did crazy things like this always happen to me?

Earl suggested that I talk to Dr. Loasby about it, and right then that made a lot of sense to me. He would surely know what to do. I rushed out to my car which was parked on the street in front of the apartment, and what a sight met my eyes. Practically every piece of glass in the car had been shattered, quite obviously by stones which still lay scattered around the automobile. What a day for troubles to be piled on my head! Fortunately, the cracked windshield did not obstruct the driver's view, so I drove to the seminary and hurried to Dr. Loasby's office. He solemnly read the letter, and told me not to worry—he would take care of everything. I tried vainly to follow that advice while watching the ushers bustle around the chapel making the final arrangements for the afternoon. I kept thinking of Lu Ann and wondering whether to alert her to the horrible possibility of what could happen during the wedding. I decided against it. After three years of engagement and planning for this moment, she must not be robbed of a happy wedding.

My reveries were interrupted by Dr. Loasby who asked me to step out in the hall with him. There Dr. D. E. Rebok, the seminary president, was waiting for us. These two men were giants in my view. Both were veterans of twenty years or more mission service in the Orient. Dr. Loasby had mastered more than one language while he labored in India, and Dr. Rebok spoke fluent Chinese from his years of distinguished service in China. They inspired confidence just by their very presence. Dr. Rebok said, "Joe, don't worry another moment about your wedding this afternoon. We have called on Miss Blank's brother and he is going to take her for a ride during the wedding. This same thing has happened before, but there will be no problem today."

I was greatly relieved, but not fully. There still might be a slip-up somewhere along the line. As soon as our conversation ended, I went back to the wedding chapel and called my ushers aside. Briefly I informed them of the problem, and gave a description of Miss Blank. By no means were they to allow her to get into the wedding or the reception. I also confided to them that the smashed windows of my car could have something to do with Miss Blank, because I had found that she lived just down the street from where the car was parked. But we had done what we could. I now began to pray most earnestly that God would not permit a disruption that could spoil this most eventful day of my life.

God answered those prayers, and the wedding went off without a hitch. No words could adequately recall and describe the emotions of that day. Lu Ann and I eluded the rice throwers who waited for us after the reception in the girls' dormitory parlor. Spirited out the back door by a friend, we were whisked to a place where my car was hidden. And by six o'clock on October 5, 1947, we were winding down Highway 66 toward Front Royal, Virginia, where our motel wedding suite was reserved for us. Another day of driving brought us to the beautiful Smoky Mountain resort at Gatlinburg, Tennessee, where we had a rustic cabin reserved for the seven-day honeymoon.

On the heels of our too-brief stay in Gatlinburg, we headed the little red car south because our first pastorate was waiting for us in Miami, Florida. We arrived there near the peak of the tourist season and found it quite impossible to find even a midget apartment for rent. After days of fruitless search, we located a twenty-eight foot house trailer that was available for an exorbitant rent. Carefully calculating the expected expenses in relation to my $34 weekly salary, we arranged for the aged trailer to be pulled in behind the little stone church on 54th Street. The members of that Hialeah congregation were wonderful and we enjoyed our short stay with them immensely. But the training program for young ministers included spending a little time with a number of experienced pastors and evangelists.

We had no furniture whatsoever, and only the household items which came through shower and wedding gifts. The more impractical items were stored away and the actual needs for apartment furnishing were easily fitted into the back of our Ford coupe. It was only slowly during those first two years that we began to accumulate beds and other furniture. Seven times within that twenty-four months we had to cram all our possessions into the trusty little car and move on to another assignment in another part of the state. Brooksville, Tampa, West Palm Beach, Lake Worth, Belle Glade, Perry and Tallahassee were called our home. In each place, in association with dedicated workers, God had something else to teach us about how to do His work and how not to do it.

In Tampa I learned one of the "don'ts" of the ministry within the first week of our arrival. Again we were forced to rent a mobile home which was permanently affixed to a mediocre trailer park near the city limits. Lu Ann had taken a special duty case at St.Joseph's Hospital to help pay off the galling automobile debt. She was working from 3:00 p.m. to 11:00 p.m., and I had attended, in spite of the rain, the graduation exercises of the church school.

The graduation took place in the sanctuary of the big Nebraska Avenue church of which I was the new assistant pastor. Afterward I visited with the guest speaker while most of the congregation scurried through the rain to their automobiles. When I left a bit later the parking lot was almost empty, and the rain was coming down harder than ever. As I pulled into the street, I noticed a woman at the bus stop in front of the church. She was trying to cover her little boy with part of her coat and watching anxiously for a bus to appear. Recognizing her as being at the graduation service, I pulled up and offered to give her a ride. She gratefully accepted, and as we rode along she recounted briefly how her non-Christian husband had persecuted her for her faith.

Soon she pointed to a service station on the left and told me that her husband was to meet her there. Because of oncoming traffic I had to let her out at another station on the opposite side, and she started across the street with her little boy in tow. As I made a U-turn in the driveway, a man came running across the road yelling for me to stop. I could see immediately that he was not only angry but he was drunk; and I correctly assumed that he was the husband of my recent passenger. Screaming curses the man yanked open the right door of my car and began to crawl inside, a long switchblade knife gleaming in his hand.

The wild verbiage had almost no sense to it, but the actions were unmistakable and clear. The one phrase which did sift through to my ears was "kill you, kill you." While scrambling out the opposite door, my tongue finally came loose and I started telling him that his wife and son were getting wet and I was trying to help them. I was a minister and thought he would appreciate a favor to his family to keep them from being soaked in the rain. Slowly a little bit of what I was saying began to seep through his drink-dulled mind. He stopped advancing and sat uncertainly with the knife upraised. Finally, as I finished the explanation the second time, he clicked the blade shut and slowly slid backwards out of the car. I slipped just as slowly back under the wheel. With a final oath he slammed the door, and staggered back across the street where his wife was fearfully watching the episode.

Later, after picking up Lu Ann at the hospital, we talked about the strange backlash of my two experiences in trying to help stranded ladies at bus stops. We finally concluded that Mr. Young Preacher had better let somebody else play Good Samaritan in such cases, unless Mrs. Young Preacher was along to add her graces.

8
Baby Boys and Stormy Weather

From Tampa we were assigned to West Palm Beach, and with all our earthly possessions packed around us in the old red Ford, we drove into West Palm in the middle of a full blown hurricane. Our four months stay there proved to be the most profitable period of my ministerial internship. In association with Evangelist Lawrence Nelson, we had the joy of working in a large tent crusade that brought scores to Christ. It was from this dedicated soulwinner that I learned the greatest methods of presenting the prophecies of Daniel and Revelation.

Following our Lake Worth Crusade, Lawrence Nelson accepted an invitation into youth work, and he turned over the tent and much of the evangelistic equipment to me. I had never held any evangelistic meetings of my own, but I knew the time had now come to launch out in faith. So, with the fresh inspiration of the Nelson meetings and most of the equipment, we moved forty miles inland to Belle Glade where I had been invited to conduct my very first crusade alone. What an experience that turned out to be! The church was very cooperative nd seemed eager to help a young aspiring evangelist make good. There was much prayer and even more hard slogging work as we cleared land for the tent.

With no helper during the ten-week series, I learned what it means to be song leader, pastor, evangelist, tent master, Bible instructor, and believe it or not, a father. Right in the middle of the crusade I had to rush Lu Ann to the hospital in Orlando, where our first son came screaming into the world at 8:14 in the morning. A few days later Larry was savoring his first tent meeting as he gurgled in his bassinet near the tent door where his mother resumed her greeting of the people.

At the end of the meetings I had the indescribable joy of baptizing eleven wonderful people who chose to follow Christ all the way. I will never forget the day I led those candidates into the Okeechobee Canal and sealed the first fruits of my evangelistic efforts. Twenty years later I would return to Florida for a state-wide camp meeting series, and the first two people to greet me on the campgrounds would be the first two souls I buried in that first baptism. Through the years they had continued to grow in the Christian life. Surely the sweetest blessings of heaven will be to meet those who were won to Christ through our influence.

From Belle Glade we moved to Perry, Florida, with the commission to raise up a completely new church in that saw-mill town. There was not a Sabbathkeeper within fifty miles, and with a small advertising budget, a wonderful lady Bible Instructor, and another young minister graduate, we launched a tent meeting right in the middle of town. The problem was that the helpers could not join me until the Sunday our crusade opened. I didn't know a soul in town so the tent erection was a special struggle. Finally on Friday it was ready to go. The freshly painted metal front stood right across the street from the Court house.

Then the radio was filled with hurricane bulletins about the season's worst storm churning up the West Coast toward Tallahassee. We were directly in the path of the 140-mile wind, and Saturday afternoon it was supposed to strike in Perry. All morning I sat in the tent praying, and watching the canvas twist under the brute force of 40-mile gusts. There was nothing I could do but pray. With no one to help me, it was impossible to lower the tent, and besides, it would have ripped the canvas to shreds even to have tried. So I just prayed, and waited, and watched, as the gusts grew stronger. Finally, about noon, I dashed across the street to a grocery store and asked what the weather report was like. "It's tearing up Cross City fifty miles south of here and coming straight at us," was the reply.

I returned to my vigil in the tent, except this time my prayers were more anguished and sincere. There was no hope at all that any of the equipment could survive the hurricane-force winds. Most of it would probably end up in the next county. I pleaded with God to give us the privilege of preaching to the souls in that town who had never heard the special prophecies of Revelation. At no time in my life had I ever felt more desperately lonely and helpless. The Bible admonition to "watch and pray" was literally what I did—watching every agonizing twist of the tent, and praying that it wouldn't get worse.

Then slowly I became conscious that the gusts seemed not so savage. It was about 2:30 p.m. when I made another dash to the store across the street. Everybody inside was talking at the same time about the latest report of the storm. It had turned inland just outside of Cross City and was following the Suwannee River towards central Florida. The worst was over as far as Perry was concerned. Our meeting would be able to open the next night on schedule. What prayers of thanksgiving we sent up that night around our family altar!

Earl Clough and Lucy Gattis arrived the next day to complete the team, and with still gusty weather we opened with fifty people inside the tent. The second Sunday night we had ninety in attendance. The third Sunday it jumped to one hundred sixty-five and a week later to two hundred twenty-five. The fifth week it hit over three hundred and we couldn't find a place for everyone on the inside. We ended the crusade with twenty-two baptisms and immediately organized the converts into a church. Twelve months later a beautiful little debt-free church building stood on the edge of town, and practically all of Taylor County was talking about it.

With Perry still in my charge, we soon moved fifty miles further north to Tallahassee, where I launched into another tent crusade. This time we were joined by another Bible instructor, Mrs. Cora Lee Barnhart, who was to influence my life to a remarkable degree. We were privileged to work with the Barnharts through three evangelistic crusades. Her dedication, love of souls, and charismatic appeal made her a joy to have on the team. She would invariably bring in fifteen, twenty or twenty-five people that she had fully prepared for baptism. Through the years she and her husband became almost like second parents to Lu Ann and me.

During our three years in Tallahassee, three extremely important things happened which shaped the direction of our future. Lu Ann gave birth to another little boy whom we named Dennis. I was permitted to stand by her during the delivery, and even though it was awesome to watch the birth, I would not choose to suffer through another. The second thing which happened was my ordination to the gospel ministry. Never will I forget the solemnity of that charge to preach God's Word, and do the work of an evangelist.

The third thing which really did bring a shake-up in our lives was a mission call to do evangelism in Bangalore, India. Aside from the momentous day of our wedding, that mission call brought the highest elation and joy. We had been in the ministry for five years waiting, wondering, and praying each year that God might lay His hands on us for foreign service. Our names had been registered with the Mission Board from the second year of college, and we had checked India as first, second, and third choice in order of preference.

It did not take us long to decide what to do about the call. Considering it an answer to prayer, we hastily wrote a letter of acceptance, and then rushed to the library to find out where Bangalore was located. The next few weeks were filled with exciting preparations—buying special supplies, selling most of our possessions, taking shots, and then saying good-bye to our families. That final farewell was the part which we had not been able to fully anticipate. Somehow, it became more difficult to face as the departure date hurried upon us.

My parents were quite old; in fact, Dad was in his early seventies and steadily failing in health. It seemed unlikely that he would survive the five years of our overseas assignment. They both wanted us to go even though the sacrifice on their part was painfully evident. Dad had only been a Christian for three years, but he longed to see the gospel preached to all the world so that Jesus could come. He had never been a man of emotion. I had never seen my father weep, but when I took him in my arms to say good-bye, his body shook with silent inward sobs that tore at my heart like a knife. I truly felt that we would not see him again until the coming of Jesus. It was the only aspect of our mission service which I ever considered a real sacrifice.

Lu Ann's parents were younger and they came to New York to see us off on the *U.S. Steel Director*, a well-fitted freighter that was to be our home for six long weeks. What mixed feelings overwhelmed us as we stood at the rail waving to those dear ones until the view was obscured. A short time later we watched the Statue of Liberty fade into the mist. Then there was nothing but water, and what water it was! Right out of New York Harbor the raging remnants of a hurricane dashed the ship unmercifully. For two days we could hardly leave the cabin. Towering waves broke against the portholes, threatening to swamp the creaking vessel at every moment.

We tied the baby's playpen to the wall so that it could not roll back and forth. Then with three-year-old Larry between us. we braced ourselves hour after hour between the wall and edge of the bunk. At times the ship would roll to such an extreme angle that it seemed to balance momentarily, shuddering in uncertainty as to whether to capsize or heel back with the next wave. We were constantly in silent prayer as the terrifying force seemed to intensify. Once, as the ship rocked with particular violence, Larry suddenly prayed aloud, "Dear Jesus, save us." How thankful we felt that he had such natural recourse to prayer in time of danger! He was mirroring our own emotions and fears and faith.

9
Introduction to India

With the passing of the storm, calm beautiful days followed our voyage through the Straits of Gibraltar, and across the Mediterranean Sea. Our first stop was Beirut, Lebanon, where Lu Ann's sister, Mary, and her husband met us. Mary and Bob preceded us to the mission field and had already served four months in Amman, the turbulent capital of the Hashemite Kingdom of Jordan, and it was a special pleasure to spend two days with them while the ship took on a new cargo. We visited the lovely campus of Middle East College, overlooking from a mountainside the blue Mediterranean.

We also found time to make a flying taxi trip to the historic ruins of Baalbec where ancient sun worship flourished in the days of Ahab and Jezebel. But too quickly the hours of shore leave sped by and we had to embark once more. A lingering stopover in Alexandria, Egypt, gave us a taxicab view of the lovely garden ground of King Farouk's summer palace. A few days later we slowly edged through the Suez Canal and anchored in the sweltering Red Sea port of Jedda, Arabia. For two miserable days we sought relief from the stifling heat while new Cadillac cars were unloaded onto the docks for the oil-rich sheiks and Arabian princes. We were fascinated also by the Moslem pilgrim ships which spewed out their human cargo for the final lap of desert travel to Mecca.

We had received a rather rude introduction to Mohammedanism earlier in our voyage from three fellow passengers, Pakistani young men who were being deported from the United States. Anxious to find out as much as possible about the Islamic religion, we had talked to them at length. One of the men had met a beautiful blond American girl in New York, who was flying to Karachi where they were to be married later in the month. Her picture was not only beautiful, but on the testimony of all three men, she was an extremely wealthy girl. The Moslem man already had one wife in his home village and the American girl would be putting on the heavy veil and joining the other wife soon after marriage. She was also surrendering her Christian faith and accepting the Moslem religion.

We were astounded that the girl was willing to accept those conditions. I asked the man, "Suppose she decides later on that she wants to be a Christian again." He answered calmly, "I would kill her." I reminded him that the American government might have something to say about one of its citizens. He said, "No, she is giving up her citizenship to become a Pakistani." With that I dropped the conversation. It was quite apparent that the men were telling the truth and I stopped trying to figure out why a beautiful, rich young American girl was taking such a foolish step.

After the Red Sea came the Indian Ocean and, at last, the sight of Bombay Harbor. With eager anticipation we scanned the crowded dock for the familiar face of Frank Ashlock, our old College Bible teacher. He had returned to India months earlier, and in a few moments we were able to recognize him, waving from the dockside. With him was Pastor Don Hunter, and what a welcome we received from those friends of long ago. This was not our point of final disembarking, but we had a full day for cargo unloading. So that night for the first time in four weeks, we slept in motionless comfort in the Ashlock's home in Poona, India.

The next morning there was only time for a quick glimpse of nearby Spicer College before we had to start driving back over the pocked trunk road to Bombay. Back on the ship we settled down for another impatient three days as we steamed past the island of Ceylon and into the Bay of Bengal. Madras was our port of entry into India, and we were weather-weary and water-weary when that destination came into view.

Again we were met by fellow missionaries who would soon seem as dear to us as members of our own families. The ship was leaving in the afternoon for Calcutta, so we had to work fast in clearing customs. There was little time for impressions or reactions until the mountainous bureaucracy of Indian paper work had been properly signed and sealed. My 1951 Chevrolet Suburban Carry-all provided the largest concern, especially when I learned that the import duty had been exactly doubled while we were on the high seas. Hastily arranging a loan from the mission office, I handed over the one hundred percent duty on the car—within pennies of what I had paid to purchase it.

It is totally impossible to portray our initial reaction to the sights, sounds, and smells in India. I must honestly record, though, that it was definitely adverse. The overwhelming impact of human beings swarming in the streets like flies, the filth, the disease, and the poverty was more than we had been prepared to meet. But the shock and revulsion melted away as we began to meet the people as individuals.

For the next five years we would continue to see beggars, dirt and disease, but we would also meet some of the finest people we had ever known—people who would become like our own family. Later, outside the cities we would view scenes of breath-taking natural beauty also. It was soon very apparent that some of our sources of information had overdrawn the picture of blight and neglected to speak of so much that was profoundly beautiful and good in India.

During the hectic week of camping in the old mission quarters in Madras, and getting our goods properly cleared through customs, I was introduced to Indian food and Indian interrupters. Neither was very appetizing at first. But let me explain that "interrupters" is just a coined word that we quickly applied to the interpreters who had to translate my sermons, sentence by sentence. How hard it was to adjust my normal rapid delivery to the painful pauses required by the "interrupters." Fortunately, our first assignment was to learn the Kanarese language double-quick so that we would not have to depend on translators any longer than necessary.

Our first encounter with the traditional rice and curry food of India took place about the third day after leaving the ship. Pastor W. F. Storz invited us to eat at the Y.M.C.A. restaurant in Madras, while we were waiting out one of the many "paper-signings" of the customs office. For years I had heard about the exotic Indian curry. A few times we had tasted a western imitation of the delicacy, which left much to be desired. Finally we were to sit down and eat the genuine article in the less-than-exotic atmosphere of an Indian restaurant.

Watching my missionary friends, I followed their example and poured the entire cup of curry on top of my plate of rice. Too late I discovered what a mistake that was. Through the years their bodies had adjusted to the high chili content of the seasoned curry, and what seemed mild to them almost burned my tongue off with the first bite. Later I learned that Madras curry is the hottest in all of India. I settled for that one spoonful, and with no boiled water at hand to relieve the burn, I suffered for the rest of the meal.

That initiation in no way discouraged me from trying again. The next few years, with weeks of itinerating through Indian villages, found me subsisting on rice and curry three times a day—and enjoying it! We found it was not a question of choice; there just wasn't much else available to eat while traveling. Fortunately, our family loved the food and found no difficulty in adapting to the rice and curry readily—the mild variety, that is.

From Madras we transferred our furnishings two hundred miles by rail to the beautiful inland city of Bangalore where our mission service would center for the next four years. There, on a 3500-foot plateau, we enjoyed one of the most ideal climates in all of Asia. With fresh fruit and vegetables available almost the year round, and living costs absolutely minimal, you probably can understand why I never counted it a sacrifice to live there. Even on the greatly reduced missionary wage scale to fit the economy of the country ($180 per month), our family of four did not find any financial hardship in making ends meet.

My first year was devoted full-time to studying the difficult Kanarese language, which was the mother tongue of about twenty million people living in Mysore State, South India. It was hard to cut back on my first love—evangelistic preaching ministry—and harder still to dig into grammar books for ten hours a day, but I knew the mission board was right in asking us to do it.

My private tutor was a former Hindu priest of a large temple near Bangalore. Everyday he bicycled to the house and spent four to six hours drilling me in the complicated construction of the language. Along with the nouns and verbs, I also received tremendous insight into the teaching and customs of the Hindu religion.

My teacher and I became very close friends. In fact, after several months I felt I could ask him a question that had puzzled me considerably about Hindu temples. Every one I had visited in South India was covered with terrible, obscene carvings. Although I knew the ancient practice of Hinduism had involved considerable carnality, including temple prostitution, I couldn't understand why the newer temples also continued to carry the erotic carvings. So I gathered my courage one day and asked the pundit, my teacher, about it.

His response was unexpected. He said, "I don't know what you're talking about." Quite taken aback by this, I invited him to step into my car for a drive down the block. A new temple had just been built down the street, and I had seen the workmen actually carving the pictures into the stone front. When he saw them, the teacher seemed to be more shocked than I was. He said, "I've never seen anything like that before, but I'll find out why and let you know tomorrow." Although I almost questioned his veracity at the time, I now believe he was telling the truth. Those carvings are so commonplace that people do not pay any attention to them.

The next day he finished our class and started to leave on his bicycle without saying anything about the carvings, so I asked him if he had found an answer to my question. He said, "Oh, yes, I found out why they put those terrible pictures on the front of temples. You see, when people go in there to worship the gods, they should not think of those evil things. So they put the pictures to remind the people not to think of those evil things when they go in to worship." I did not offend my teacher by even a sign of amusement, but later Lu Ann and I had a good laugh over the answer. As though anyone would ever need to be reminded by evil not to think of evil!

After six months of language study the teacher felt that I was ready to take the first year examination. A regular interdenominational school operated in Bangalore for missionaries of all faiths, but the board had felt that I could make more rapid progress through private study. The time had come to find out. The annual oral and written language tests were reputed to be rigorous in the extreme. I tried to prepare, and my pundit drilled me unmercifully, but I felt absolutely terrified by that ordeal. Conversation in the oral section would be all in Kanarese, and the teachers could ask me to relate any incident or parable from the Bible that they might choose. I remembered how tense I had been during my orals for the Master's degree, but it didn't compare with the torture I went through anticipating that language board exam.

The written part was not bad, but I was sweating my way through the oral conversation part with considerable difficulty. Then the solemn Indian professor asked me to relate the story of the Prodigal Son in Kanarese. My heart sang, because that had been the one story I completely mastered. I had even prepared a little sermonette in Kanarese built around that parable. I believe to this day that it was only that fortuitous circumstance which gave me a passing grade, and made me one of the very few who ever passed the first year exams after only six months' study. Many missionaries had to study a full second year to make the grade. God's blessing and a good teacher gave me an advantage for which I was ever so grateful.

10
Veiled Trouble and Mistaken for a King

During the first year of full-time study, I carried the weekend pastoral responsibilities of the large Bangalore church. Besides preaching on Sabbath, I had almost no other congregational duties. I did have to visit the church treasurer occasionally to keep the finances in order. The first visit I made to his house brought me into an exciting adventure that I would never care to repeat.

One evening at dusk I drove into the Moslem street where the treasurer, Mr. DeJong, had recently rented a house. All the houses were surrounded by high walls and gates because the Mohammedan women were kept secluded from public view and contact. When they did appear on the street it was in purdah; that is, completely covered from head to foot with a heavy veil, called a burkah. Even their eyes were not always visible through the small slot in the veil.

The treasurer's high gate had been pointed out to me and I thought I knew exactly which one it was. So I opened it and walked across the compound. Then I heard a terrible scream. I looked up to see a woman in the doorway. She had a look of pure terror on her face, and seemed almost paralyzed by my presence. I knew immediately that it was the wrong house, so I rushed back through the gate. I quickly discovered that Mr. DeJong lived in the next house, so I entered that gate. But his wife informed me that he was not at home.

Coming back to the street I was suddenly surrounded

by an angry group of men demanding to know why I had come into their compound. I'm sure I was visibly shaken by the threatening attitude of the group, and only my foreign visitor status saved me from serious consequences. After repeated explanations and apologies, I was permitted to get in my car. But within a block another group of hostile men stepped into the road and forced me to stop. They had been searching for me in the other direction, and I had to go through all my former explanations. Reluctantly and sullenly they finally allowed me to drive away. I had surely learned another precious lesson about how to respect the fanatic religious feelings of the Moslem community. It was altogether probable that I had looked into the face of a woman who, since teenage, had not been seen by another man outside her own family.

During my second year of part-time study I was able to start holding evangelistic meetings in the city of Bangalore. That was the beginning of some of the most thrilling years of my ministry. About twelve Indian young people of college age joined me as helpers in some of the tent crusades I conducted. As pastor of the church, I had learned to appreciate those young people especially. They loved my three-seater Suburban Carry-all and had nicknamed it "Brother Van." I sometimes packed as many as seventeen into the old Chevy, for special outings with those youth helpers.

In the ten-week series the girls served as usherettes and provided music. The boys helped care for the tent, led music, and helped visit some of the interests. It was terrific! An entire volume could be packed with the stories of God's grace at work in the lives of those who were won to Christ in those meetings. Two young Hindu lads were baptized who went on to study for the ministry. One of them was beaten and disowned by his family, and he is still the only member of his family who is not a Hindu today.

Samuel is now a Christian worker in Poona, India.

The other boy graduated from Spicer College at the head of his class, married a lovely girl from Ceylon and went to that island field to preach. Years later he came to America to earn his Master's degree and Bachelor of Divinity degree. At the time I was pastor of a large church in Louisville, Kentucky, and Jacob brought his family to visit me. What a thrill it was to listen to him preach a powerful evangelistic message in my church! As he held six hundred people spellbound that day, my mind went back to the Bangalore Tent Crusade; and all I could see was that young, barefoot boy sitting wide-eyed on the front seat, drinking in the glorious message of the gospel. What a miracle of God's transforming grace!

One of the most unusual things happened to me one day as I drove toward the Bangalore train station to pick up tickets for an upcoming trip. My route led along Station Road and intersected the wide Mahatma Gandhi Boulevard near the center of town. As I neared the boulevard I could see that the intersection was completely blocked by thousands of people who were waiting to get a glimpse of the visiting King of Arabia. King Saud was due at any moment for an official state visit to Bangalore. The beautiful main avenue had been sealed off and huge signs stretched over the street emblazoned with the words, WELCOME KING SAUD. Police held back the solid phalanx of people who craned and shoved to get a favorable view of the anticipated route of the royal procession. Many had their own banners and flags in hand with which to welcome the visiting monarch.

Unable to get through the intersection, I resigned myself to waiting out the arrival of the king. There was no way to reach the station without crossing Mahatma Gandhi Boulevard. Fifteen minutes passed and the restless crowd still waited. Finally it occurred to me that the crowds might thin out further toward the edge of town, so I drove along a parallel street for several blocks and came back up to the boulevard. My heart sank as I saw the mass of people and police waiting there just like the other place.

After ten more impatient minutes I appealed to the nearby policeman to please help me get across the avenue. I reminded him that it was most urgent for me to get to the railroad station, and that obviously something had happened to delay the arrival of the entourage. The policeman was sympathetic, but seemed uncertain about what to do. I suggested that he could separate the crowd and just let me drive across the boulevard, but he pointed out that he could not leave his assigned position to open up the way for me on the other side of the street.

Finally, though, as the minutes dragged by and no procession appeared, he told me that he would make a path for me to enter the avenue, and that I should drive the five blocks back to Station Road and get off there. That was more than I expected and I was elated to drive out into the broad deserted boulevard. I started driving my rattle-trap old van down the street underneath the welcome banners, and suddenly the crowd went wild. They began to scream and wave their handkerchiefs. They thought I was the King of Arabia! And for five blocks and about five minutes I got everything that King Saud got as he came along a few minutes later. What a sensation it was to view that sea of faces looking at me and shouting for my attention as though I were the most important person in all the world! Looking back on the experience later I was thankful that the king had no political enemies lying in wait to assassinate him along the route. Certainly I learned one great lesson that day—things are not always what they seem to be.

Between evangelistic crusades, I served for a time as president of the mission work in the Kanarese section of

South India. This entailed much travel, often weeks at a time, into the remote village areas where small churches flourished. Sometimes the villages were accessible by train, but often they could be reached only by bicycle or ox cart. In company with J. Daniel, my pastor translator, I would tour the circle of churches, holding special services to encourage the members and strengthen the pastors. Often we conducted baptisms for those who were ready for that important step.

After returning from those village itineraries I had thrilling stories to tell Lu Ann about the spiritual conquests, and sometimes about the physical dangers also. There were problems of eating and drinking, because all drinking water had to be boiled. Most village drinking water was taken out of rivers where animals and people had taken their baths.

On one tour Daniel and I had to rent bicycles for a particularly rugged ride through several miles of jungle trail to visit an isolated village church. Never having ridden bicycles as a child, I found it especially uncomfortable to bounce over the narrow winding path. We closed the evening meeting in the little thatch-roof mud church about ten o'clock and began to make preparations for the return trip. The pastor was alarmed at our plans to cycle back through the jungle at night, because it was the special hunting area of the Maharajah of Mysore, and no one ventured there at night due to the presence of tigers, leopards and other animals of prey.

We had to meet another appointment the following day, and felt it imperative to return that night. Nevertheless, we were thrown into a dilemma of uncertainty after the pastor told us what had happened a few days earlier. A cow belonging to one of the church members had wandered into the jungle and he had gone with some of the members to find the cow. As they were bringing the cow out of the jungle, a tiger suddenly sprang from the bushes, knocking the pastor to the ground. The cow ran one way and the church members ran another way. When the pastor got up, unhurt, the tiger crouched in front of him, ready to spring. He stood stock-still looking the tiger in the eye. For thirty minutes, he told us, the tiger did not move and neither did he. The members wept and prayed from a safe distance thinking his doom was sealed. Finally, after an estimated half hour, the tiger roared and stalked off into the underbrush. I say "estimated" because I seriously don't believe the episode lasted that long. Surely it must have seemed more than that to the terrified pastor. It might have been only a few minutes.

But regardless of the time, that was the same jungle we had to cycle through to get back to our bed rolls and to catch an early train the next morning. Reluctantly we mounted our bikes and to our dismay, discovered that Daniel's light would not even give a flicker. It was completely dead. In desperation we decided to have him follow closely behind my cycle, as we covered the return twelve miles or so.

Probably I have never passed a more miserable night in all my life than that one turned out to be. In the first place, we were scared, knowing full well that wild animals were in the very same area in which we were traveling. In the second place, I was not an expert rider, and my flickering little light only hit the tops of the ridges and bumps. Over and over I fell off the bike and Daniel came crashing into me in the darkness. Finally the dynamo on my cycle broke and we had no light at all.

I never knew the night could be so dark nor the jungle so noisy. There were cries and calls and sounds of movement. You can be sure our imaginations worked overtime as we struggled to tie the dynamo back in place with my handkerchief. Finally, in the pitch blackness, we managed a temporary repair that had to be repeated every few minutes.

I thought that night would never end. I was black and blue from falling, and ached from head to foot from tension, bruises and general misery. Sometime in the wee hours of the morning the first lights of Chamrajnagar came into view, and it was the happiest sight I thought I had ever seen. We staggered into the traveler's bungalow where we had left our bed rolls and fell onto the wooden benches for a brief sound sleep. It seemed only a moment before the sun woke us up barely in time to wash our faces and catch the train for our next appointment.

Later that same year I had another experience of providential deliverance while on a train trip from Travancore. The workers from my Kanarese Section were meeting with the pastors in the Malayalam Section for an evangelistic institute. The meeting was held in Kottarakarra, deep in the lush coastal area of Travancore State. After the institute I boarded a train for the overnight trip back to Bangalore. Indian trains are divided into compartments which do not connect with each other. They can only be entered from the outside. At night, the sitting bunks are turned into sleeping bunks in the second-class compartments. I felt fortunate to be in a compartment to myself where I anticipated getting a good night's sleep. I hoped that no one would get into my compartment as the train made its myriad stops at village stations along the way.

Technically the doors were supposed to be left unlocked all night just in case a passenger wanted to get into the compartment. But as darkness fell it seemed more than likely that I would have the bunks to myself that night. As I walked over to turn on the light I also bolted the outside doors on both sides of the compartment. A moment later as I resumed my seat, the train suddenly slowed to a crawl and then a jarring halt. For some reason the train had stopped in the middle of a jungle area.

As I watched out the window in the growing dusk, I saw a man walk out of the jungle and look quickly up and down the train. I saw him look at me intently. Then with a wild dash he leaped from the embankment and grabbed the handle of my compartment door. As he twisted it, I jumped up and ran to the door. He was hanging onto the side of the train, and wrenching the handle with all his strength. His face was against the bars on the door window, and never to my dying day can I forget the hatred and evil on that face as he literally snarled at me. When he realized that the door was locked, he threw me a final look of rage and jumped from the train. I could barely see him fleeing into the jungle as the train began to move again.

Only then did I fully sense what had taken place. It had all happened so quickly that I had no time to be frightened. The newspaper often reported the activities of bandits who would enter train compartments where Europeans or Americans were traveling alone. Knifing them to death, they would take their luggage and money and disappear into the jungle in a few moments. The crime would go undetected for hours, or until another passenger entered the compartment. There was usually no way for the bandit to be apprehended. A missionary nurse had been murdered in exactly the same manner only a few weeks earlier.

I offered a prayer of thanksgiving as the train lurched onward in the dark. I now understood why I had locked those doors just minutes before the man leaped onto the train. Surely the Lord had moved me to take that small action which probably saved my life. Someday in God's kingdom I want to talk to my guardian angel and find out exactly what would have happened had he not led me to lock that door.

11
Attacked by a Hindu Mob

During the third year of mission service we were assigned to break into one of the most forbidding cities of South India with the saving message of Christ. Plans included a large-scale public crusade in the very heart of Mysore City, and a long-range follow-up program to establish a church. It was felt that we should actually move the family and make Mysore our home for at least a year. We were excited at the plans, because that beautiful city was one of the most fascinating places in the country as far as we were concerned. It was largely a Hindu center. There were very few Christian churches in the city, except one large Catholic cathedral and a small Methodist congregation.

The palace of the Maharajah of Mysore dominated the majestic boulevards which fanned out like spokes from a central hub, the fantastic oriental palace looked exactly like a fabled Arabian Nights with tiered gold-covered domes. During certain weeks of the year the palace glowed under the all-night illumination of light bulbs spaced only inches apart over the entire building. There are no words to describe the breathtaking spectacle. I have never seen anything in the West which equaled the grandeur of that palace.

We rented a house from a famous Indian surgeon who was transferring to Bangalore to become medical director of Victoria Hospital. The house had a magnificent yard and garden area, and more rooms than we could ever think of using, but it was all we could locate to rent after weeks of searching. For several weeks, in fact, we occupied a house which had no indoor plumbing and a very limited water supply. What a contrast when we finally settled into the sprawling old mansion on Viceroy Road.

There was much preparation work to be done before the big public crusade, and I was extremely grateful for the four young Indian pastors who had become part of the team. As usual, J. Daniel would be doing the translating for me. Although he was quite young, Daniel had a lot of talent and was always pleasant to work with. Neither of us had any way of knowing that our most harrowing evangelistic experience was about to begin.

After much negotiating with the municipal council, we were able to lease the facilities of the beautiful Town Hall for the ten-week series. Besides being the largest and most commodious auditorium in town, it was situated directly across the street from the fabulous Maharaja's palace. Surely no more prestigious building could have been secured anywhere. The only immediate disadvantage seemed to be the huge twenty-foot pictures of Hindu gods which lined the walls from front to back. Figuring that we could easily arrange their temporary removal, we signed the lease contract and proceeded with the city-wide advertising schedule.

We hired boys to distribute thousands of handbills door to door just a week before the opening night. Only then did we learn why the pictures were in the Town Hall. The fanatic Hindu Mahasabah political party used the building as their area headquarters, and they were fiercely opposed to all foreign influence in India. As a religious party, they hated missionaries and felt that Christians fomented disloyalty to the Hindu government. It had been one of their members who assassinated Gandhi because they feared he was leaning towards the Christian religion.

For two years the government had outlawed the party, but now it had grown back stronger than ever.

We were alerted to trouble when the boys distributing the handbills reported being attacked by thugs who tore up their handbills and told them that I would never be permitted to preach in their auditorium. We were dismayed at that turn of events but it was already too late to make any change in the crusade plans.

Later in the week the Indian pastor of the little Methodist church came to visit me. He had heard the rumblings and wanted to warn of the personal dangers we faced. For years no Christian group in the city of Mysore had been able to hold any religious meetings outside of their church building. Every time it had been tried the Hindu Mahasabah had stoned the meeting and forced the worshippers to flee. Innocently, we had not only scheduled services outside a church, but right in the headquarters building of the fanatical opposition. It only added to my apprehension when the pastor solemnly assured me that his church would be praying for me every Sunday morning!

The undercurrent of rumor and report grew louder as the opening night approached. My Indian helpers assured me that most of the city was buzzing over the unprecedented situation. We hurried to the auditorium that first night with some very mixed feelings, but what a sight met our eyes! The hall was packed to the doors with over eleven hundred people. At least twelve uniformed police were stationed all around the aisles of the auditorium. Apparently they had heard about the threatenings of the Mahasabah party and were there to protect us.

In spite of some peripheral disorder the service went fairly smoothly. We sensed a segment of hostility in the middle front section of the audience, but the watchful police did not move from the aisles even during the sermon. For eight nights the seats were packed and the police were on hand. I would preach the sermon in English for the fifty percent of listeners who could understand it, and then Daniel would give the same message in Kanarese. No one left between the services although it was obvious that half of them were hearing the same thing through twice.

Almost nightly after the benediction, several men would surround us at the front and try to engage in a political dialogue. I would gently explain that my work was religious and refuse to be drawn into any such discussions. But we could see flashes of anger and resentment in their faces. After three or four nights, Daniel began to meet hostile knots of men who railed at him for serving as my translator. I instructed all four of the young ministers to ride their cycles together to the quarters where they all had rooms, and never separate under any condition. It had become very obvious that Daniel's safety was being threatened. Often the boys would have to sneak out the back of the Town Hall because the gang of opposers was running to the front gate shouting, "Get Daniel! Get Daniel!"

On the eighth night after the meeting, Lu Ann and I dropped off the wives of the two married workers at their house as we did each evening. Driving back through the near-deserted streets we met three of the workers on their cycles, but Daniel was not with them. We stopped to find out where he was and they informed us that the light had burned out on his cycle. Since it was illegal to ride at night with no light, he had to start pushing his bicycle. Fortunately they were quite near home, and the three had decided it was safe to leave him behind.

Anxiously we drove on along the street watching for Daniel. Suddenly our headlights picked out a little group of men beside the road, and at the last moment, we recognized Daniel in the middle of the circle. Quickly braking to a halt, I jumped out and ran back to the men. They fell back in dismay as I broke into the group and asked what was going on. One of them muttered that Daniel was going with them to explain some things. I told them that I would explain anything that needed explaining. Without any further word they ran and jumped into a car that was parked nearby.

A relieved young translator helped me tie his cycle on the back of my old van while we kept a wary eye on the other automobile. Apparently they were waiting to follow my car to find out where Daniel lived. As I started moving, the other car also started, but I made a quick U-turn in the street and dashed down a small cluttered alley. It was too late for the other car to get turned to follow even if it had been driven by an expert. A few highly accelerated twists and turns and we were quite certain the other car could never follow us. Dropping Daniel and his bicycle as quickly as possible, we sped away to get out of the neighborhood just in case the pursuers had picked up our trail.

In our workers' meeting the next morning all of us sensed that opposition was intensifying on the part of the Hindu Mahasabah. The Indian pastors could recognize that about two hundred of the audience each night belonged to the most violent wing of the party. We prayed earnestly for God to overrule and to give us wisdom for every move. I was mostly concerned for Daniel's safety, and even though he maintained a courageous front, I knew he had been shaken considerably by the events of the previous night. We agreed that for the rest of the crusade Daniel should be driven to his home in the van after each service.

As we came into the auditorium that night we were gratified to see the same overflow crowd of people, practically all of them Hindus. Up to that ninth night we had made contact with scores of the people in their homes, and knew of the genuine interest they had in the truths we were preaching. Many of them were weary of the empty worship of mud gods and were eagerly drinking in their first knowledge of a living God who loved them. We felt that eighty percent of the listeners were sincere seekers for the truth, and they were all in their places waiting for the singing to begin. But suddenly we were struck by the fact that the police were not in their place! In fact, only one subinspector was anywhere to be seen in the auditorium that night. I sought him out and asked where the rest of our uniformed friends were. He said, "Prime Minister Nehru is in town and it is his birthday. Four thousand children are giving him a birthday party in the park and all the police were called there to control the crowd."

Just then one of the pastors hurried up to me and whispered that several of the men were carrying bags of stones as they came into the auditorium. It was immediately apparent that the trouble-makers had been waiting for this night when the police would be involved elsewhere, and they were prepared for action. I knew without doubt that this night was the showdown. The only thing we didn't know was just how they would initiate the attack.

With a great deal of apprehension inside, but with outward calm I came to the end of my English sermon, and Daniel began to speak. As though on signal a young man sprinted down the center aisle and jumped onto the platform. Later we learned he was a Communist agitator hired to do the work of disruption with which he was so familiar.

I stood up to meet him, and he tried to place a paper in my hand containing a long list of loaded political questions. In a loud voice he challenged me to answer the questions. I ignored the paper and spoke into the microphone, reminding the audience that we could not answer questions from the floor but would gladly meet anyone after the meeting. Then the youth began to shout to the audience and about two hundred others jumped to their feet in the front center section. In practiced cadence they began to chant slogans under the direction of the man on the platform. He would shout "Hindu Mahasabah!," and they would scream back, "Jai!," which means "victory." The purpose, of course, was to completely drown out any more preaching by the din of constant shouting.

I got very close to the microphone and called for the one policeman to come forward and remove the man from the platform. The sub-inspector, though an officer, was afraid to do anything. Generally the police of India command little respect and exercise very little authority. Finally, after repeated encouragement he reluctantly came and led the young man away. That seemed to be a sign for the two hundred hecklers to attack the pulpit. They began to swarm over the seats toward the platform.

I whispered to Daniel to get out the back door and into my car. As he disappeared through the massive curtains which were kept drawn as a backdrop, the first wave of demonstrators scrambled up onto the stage. But at that same moment out of the corner of my eye, I saw a man rush up from the far left of the platform. He reached my side and grabbed the microphone out of my hand. He began to shout to the audience in Kanarese, and only then did I recognize him as the Mayor of the city who had negotiated with us for the rental of the auditorium. Apparently everyone else recognized the Mayor also, because the bedlam subsided almost instantly and the agitators stopped their advance.

Through the providence of God he had walked into the hall to use a public phone just as the demonstration broke out, and had seen my danger.

While he appealed to the crowd, I slipped back through the curtains to pick up my recorder and projector which I greatly feared might be smashed by the fanatics. Then, with the equipment in hand, I walked back across the platform, into the crowd, and toward the front door. I gambled that the Mayor could keep them occupied while I made it to the door, but above everything else, I was determined to show no fear of them. It would have been simple to slip out the back door, but I wanted them to know we were not being intimidated by their threats.

The crowd parted before me to make a path, and for a moment, it seemed that they were too stunned to act. But then the whole room exploded into action. It appeared that the entire group fell in at my heels shouting, "Down with Christianity! Down with foreign missionaries!" By the time I reached the car Lu Ann and the children were safely inside, and so were all four of my helpers. Daniel was trembling with a justified fear for his very life.

With the doors closed and locked I began to worm the car slowly through the sullen crowd. They fell back to give a barely adequate exit lane, but kicks, blows, rocks, and sticks rained upon all sides of the car as we passed through the gauntlet and pulled into the open street. With heavy hearts we made our way home that night, full of uncertainty as to what the next day would bring forth.

The next morning I was waited upon very early by a messenger from the Mayor's office, asking me to see him at the earliest possible moment. Postponing the workers' meeting for an hour, I hurried down to find the Mayor and two of his leading counselors waiting for me. They came to the point immediately. The lease contract on the Town Hall was now null and void, and we were strictly forbidden to have another meeting there. I reasoned and pleaded with the men, and they were sympathetic, realizing that it was not our fault that the trouble erupted, but they were adamant in the decision to close the crusade. They said that bloodshed would be inevitable if we held even one more meeting.

Sadly I had to carry the news to the waiting workers, and while we prayed that morning we also wept over those hundreds of sincere Hindu friends who would no longer be able to hear the truth presented. It was one of the greatest disappointments I had ever met in evangelism, but it was only an omen of a still greater disappointment that would later grow out of the same experience. That evening we drove to the Town Hall and saw it ringed with policemen, turning away the hundreds who were seeking entrance.

Happily, the crusade was not a complete failure, because I was able to visit a number of the interested ones whom we had come to know at the auditorium. A few weeks later we had a baptism for several who made their decision right in the home. We gave them Bible studies and prepared them for entrance into the body of Christ.

12 Government Orders "Get Out!"

Shortly after the crusade was closed down, Lu Ann gave birth to our third child, who also turned out to be our third son. Ronnie was born at the little Wesleyan Mission Hospital, which was staffed by the only overseas doctor in town. In fact, the English lady doctor and her nurse were the only Europeans living within one hundred miles of Mysore, and we were the only Americans in the city.

I must confess to some disappointment when the nurse brought out another baby boy. Having been deprived of sisters, I had always anticipated having a little daughter someday to make up for the loss. Another missionary family from Bangalore had been expecting their third child about the same time—the Shepherds. They had two daughters already, and naturally wanted a boy the next time. Well, you guessed it! They had a third daughter and we had a third son. But he was healthy and handsome (like his mother) so I was very thankful.

After living in Mysore for almost a year and overseeing the mission work throughout the Kanarese field, I began to hunger for more public evangelism. My knowledge of the language had grown considerably during the year we lived in Mysore, because few of the uneducated people could speak English, and I was forced to communicate with them in their own tongue. I felt that within another year I would be able to preach my first full sermon in Kanarese. It was an exciting thought.

In the meantime it seemed wise to move back to Bangalore where I could hold another ten-week crusade in English. Because of the British occupation influence the majority of Bangaloreans could understand enough English to enjoy the evangelistic messages. Instead of settling in the Cantonment area where most of the other missionaries lived and where most foreigners also resided, we moved into Bangalore City, a section almost exclusively occupied by Indian families.

Immediately we started laying the groundwork for another public crusade. The same beautiful tent was available that we had used for the first Bangalore series two years earlier. After much searching for a suitable place on which to erect the tent, we came to the conclusion that no spot could equal the one we had used before. So, unusual as it was, we rented the same large lot at No. 2 Residency Road for the second time. It was ideally located on a central avenue, and very easy to identify on the advertising leaflets. Many people also remembered the previous series and were eager to attend another on the same location.

The young people associated with me in even a stronger way, and every indication pointed toward an ideal campaign. Some very fine young ministers joined our workers' team. Attendance was even better than before and often we had people standing outside the tent or sitting on the ground to hear the message. Again we were gratified to see large numbers of non-Christians attending the crusade.

Experience had taught me a treat deal about the keen philosophic minds of the educated Hindu class. They were versed in logic and metaphysical gymnastics. Time and again I tried to argue them into accepting the Christian doctrine, but with little success. Their analytical mentality dredged up subtle arguments that I had never heard of, and which soon persuaded me that it was hopeless to philosophize with them. I found that the only way to really win a Hindu to Christ was through the avenue of love. Their minds were geared to operate on a different wavelength from a Westerner, but their hearts were just as easily moved as our own.

Two weeks before the crusade began I was attending a tremendous rally at the Bangalore Central College where Nehru was making a speech. Over two hundred thousand people were massed on the cricket field, seated on the ground, but loud speakers easily carried the words of the prime minister to every corner of the mammoth outdoor audience. I happened to be seated by a Hindu young man who was a student at the college. He was very nationalistic and manifested an almost fanatical pride in everything that was Indian. We conversed at some length on a very friendly basis until he asked me what work I was doing in India. The moment he understood that I was a missionary, his whole attitude changed. He angrily and loudly began to denounce the work of Christian missions, and asked why I had come to try to change their Hindu religious beliefs. He said, "The government ought to send every missionary out of the country."

I calmly tried to explain to the young man that we had not come to force religion on anyone. We had simply found something that brought great peace and happiness and wanted to share it with others. I reminded him that India was a democratic country similar to my own, and all had a right to speak their beliefs to others, whether Hindu or Christian. But in his agitated state I wasn't sure that anything was really getting through to him.

When the meeting was over and the final ovation for Prime Minister Nehru had died away, I hurriedly explained to the young man that I would be starting a special series of talks in two weeks. With tongue in cheek,

I invited him to attend the tent meetings at No. 2 Residency Road. He reacted with distaste, as I feared he would, and bade me a curt and cool good-bye. I was troubled that the visit had been so unsatisfying, and especially so since he harbored such bitter feelings toward the missionaries. I had no reason at all to believe that I would ever see the young man again.

But I was wrong. I did see him again. On the seventh night of the crusade I preached on the great plan of salvation, dwelling at length on the love of God in giving His Son to die for our sins. As I greeted the people thronging out of the tent that night, a youth grabbed my hand and squeezed it with both of his. He said, "You probably don't remember me, but you talked to me at the Nehru rally. I'm not a Christian, I'm a Hindu. But I'm miserable and I'm going to do what you said tonight." There were tears in his eyes. In the crush of the crowd I only had time to assure him of God's love for him.

I watched for the boy after that, and he was always present and on time. His name was Prasad and he brought fellow students with him to fill an entire row, and listened intently to every sermon. But alas, that man nor any of his friends would ever be able to hear that series out. Right in the middle of the crusade I received orders from the government of India to be out of the country within thirty days. I was not permitted to continue the meetings beyond the fifth week.

I must tell you what led up to that traumatic government directive in a moment, but first let me tell you about my Hindu student friend. When I made the announcement to the tent audience, it was like a thunder bolt had fallen. At the close of the meeting that night, Prasad rushed up and asked if I would object to his getting up a petition in my behalf. I assured him it would be all right with me. The following night was the final service in the tent, and at the end of that emotional evening, Prasad brought to me a petition with almost six hundred signatures which he had gathered that day and evening. It was one of the most moving appeals I had ever read. Eloquently he presented to the government officers his personal reasons for wanting missionaries to stay in India. This was the same student who had railed against Christians and who wanted all missionaries deported immediately. What had happened? He had heard about a God who loved him. In contrast to the corrupt consort-gods of Hinduism, here was one that provoked love instead of fear. His mind was just as philosophical as ever, but his heart had been broken by the knowledge of Christ's love and sacrifice for him.

Unhappily, this time I had no opportunity to stay by and follow up the interest personally. I can only pray and trust that those seeds of truth were nourished in good soil, and that they sprang up into a newborn Christian experience. What a joy it will be if I meet Prasad in the Kingdom of God and learn the rest of the story of God's grace in his life. I believe that will be a part of my reward in that Paradise to come.

Now let me return a moment to the circumstances which led to the government orders to leave India. Early in the Bangalore series I had applied for the regular extension of stay which is required of all foreigners in India. Permission is granted routinely. But this time, in my case, the directive came back that my extension of stay was granted only for thirty days, at the end of which I had to be out of the country. Ironically, I overlooked the plain government envelope after it arrived in the mail and left it lying unopened for two precious days of my allotted thirty.

From the moment I read the "quit India" orders, I sought in every conceivable way to have the decision rescinded. The Division and local mission authorities made petition to the government. Hindu groups and Christian groups made inquiry, but the only explanation offered officially was that there was a breach of peace in my Mysore meetings; therefore, I was undesirable in the country. For days I could only feel bitter grief and even resentment that we should be so unjustly singled out for something we had no responsibility for. But soon we reconciled to the comforting assurance that all things work together for good to those that love God. Though we could see no possible reason for our work to be cut just when I was ready to begin using the language which had cost me two years of life, yet we resigned to God's will and direction.

The hardest part was to leave the people that we had learned to love so deeply. How could we part with those dedicated young people—Pauline, Russell, Ena, Carol, Janet, David and a dozen more who had given their time and talents to helping win souls? And what of the scores whom we had baptized and who were still so dependent on our encouragement?

Another real concern to us was the fact that our regular five-year term of service would not expire for another fifteen months. We dreaded the thought of returning to the homeland before we had fulfilled the terms of our assignment. Letters began to fly back and forth between Bangalore and Poona, our Division office. The country of Pakistan was also under the same mission committee, and it was soon explained to us that an evangelist was needed in Lahore, West Pakistan. Would we consider moving two thousand miles north and complete the rest of our term? The people there were mostly Mohammedan, and we had received some early unpleasant impressions of that religious group. But after praying together over the invitation, Lu Ann and I both felt that we should accept it as the call of God.

More letters sailed back and forth, and the arrangements were finalized that we would sell most of our furnishings and proceed to Lahore by train. A thirty-day government extension was granted us at the last minute for the multitudinous details of sorting, selling and packing for the move. The very thought of the task overwhelmed us. The trip itself would take almost a week on the slow Indian trains, and three small boys did not make the prospect any easier to contemplate. We would have to sell our well-worn but dependable "Bro. Van" as well as most of the electrical appliances. Somehow the electrical systems of Pakistan did not jibe with what we had, and most of the household things would have to be disposed of.

At least the extension of time gave me a little opportunity to work with souls who were preparing for baptism. One man, in particular, had made his decision under great difficulties, and I had learned to love that man very much. He was a Parsi gentleman by the name of Mr. Tarrapore, and he did not miss a night during the time we were able to hold the meetings. As a follower of the Zoroastrian religion, Mr. Tarrapore worshiped fire as his chief god. But I noticed, in visiting his beautiful home, that there were many other gods in niches all around the walls of the living room. The little eternal flame burned on the mantel day and night to symbolize faith in the god of fire above all the others.

Every Sunday morning I would visit Mr. Tarrapore, and almost every week another one of the niches in the wall would be empty. Slowly the gods were taken out of the house, until finally, only the god of fire remained on the mantel piece. Never will I forget the morning when I entered the home and found the fire gone from its place.

The following Sunday another thrilling step was taken in conforming to the Christian faith. I had preached the night before on the Lord's Supper, and the beautiful ordinance of footwashing which Jesus commanded. As soon as I entered the home, Mr. Tarrapore excused himself and returned in a moment with a pan of water. He asked if he could wash my feet, and with tears streaming down his face he knelt to tenderly wash my feet. I can never forget that scene because of what it signified of that prominent bank official.

It meant one thing to me. Mr. Tarrapore was a born-again Christian. In India the feet are considered very unclean. The most demeaning thing is to touch another person's shoes or feet. Only the lowest outcasts, or untouchables, would lower themselves to making deliberate contact with anyone's feet. Yet there was the high caste gentleman, following the example of Jesus, and washing my feet with his tears. It was a sight I have never forgotten. It proved to me that he was every whit a Christian. He objected when I insisted on washing his feet, and I had to remind him again of the instruction Jesus gave that we "should wash one another's feet." He sat and wept while I reciprocated in the precious ordinance of humility. I must confess that my tears flowed that day also. Never has the experience of footwashing meant so much to me as it did in that private home service when Mr. Tarrapore took the final step in his commitment to follow the Saviour all the way. How sad it is that so many millions of church members miss the blessing intended for them by disobeying the three-fold command of Jesus concerning footwashing.

Saying good-bye to the land of India was one of the saddest days of my life. About a hundred of our closest friends, including many that we had baptized. came to the train station in Bangalore to see us off. I knew that there was little chance of seeing any of them again until we met them in God's kingdom. Mr. Tarrapore was there, and some of his Hindu business friends who had attended our meetings also. Many of the people brought garlands and we were almost weighted down by the flowers around our necks. As the train began to move the group started singing, "God Be With You 'Till We Meet Again." Lu Ann and I were both trying to hide our tears as those strains of song faded into the distance. It required all the faith we could muster to accept this move as a part of God's will. After years of language study, now apparently wasted, it seemed so frustrating to leave it all behind. But we knew that somewhere up ahead we would find the answers, and understand why God was permitting that bitter experience.

13
Pakistan Tragedy

The monotonous rail trip north was broken by a stopover in New Delhi where friends escorted us to the incomparable Taj Mahal. In the near-border town of Amritsar we visited the beautiful gold-leafed temple which constitutes the nerve center of the bearded Sikh religious group.

The actual border crossing involved quite a bit of red tape and wasted motion. The governments of India and Pakistan had been skirmishing almost daily in spite of U.N. sanctions and inspections. The trucks carrying our furnishings were halted at the edge of a no-man's land, and all boxes were shifted to the heads of twenty Indian coolies. Under the watchful eye of heavily armed guards on both sides of the neutral strip, we had to walk the quarter mile to a central checkpoint. There we were met by twenty Pakistani coolies who took the load the rest of the way into the Pakistani customs building. In spite of advance agreement on the price per coolie, endless haranguing always developed as the loads shifted from one head to another. The traditional "baksheesh," or tip, is much more entrenched in the Orient than in our western society.

Fortunately, new missionary friends were waiting just outside the customs house to oversee the rental of Pakistani trucks to transport our battered goods on their final lap to Lahore. Bitter enmity between the two countries had almost eliminated any cooperation in mutual trade or import agreements. We had been told already, for example, that there would be no more bananas available as soon as we crossed the border.

Luscious and cheap on one side, they were impossible to obtain at any price just a mile away. We took the maximum allowable with us as visa holders, and resigned ourselves to the near fresh fruitless diet of the desert Punjab country.

We arrived at our new home in Lahore, Pakistan, just as the winter cold was dropping the nighttime temperatures to 40 degrees or less. With no way of heating the house with its high ceiling and open architecture, we shivered through the unfamiliar cold of the first winter. In contrast to the year round ideal climate of Bangalore, the Pakistan spring and summer temperature rapidly escalated to 100 degrees, then to 110 degrees and finally to almost 120 degrees. We understood then why the ceilings were high.

Within a month after our arrival in Pakistan, we passed through another emotional crisis in our family which almost led to our immediate return to the United States. It involved our oldest son, Larry, who was seven years old at the time. He adapted quickly to the new environment and soon had made fast friends with the little boy who lived next door to us. Ashraf's father was one of the Pakistani pastors who had been converted from Islam a few years earlier and had become a dynamic leader of Christian work in the Punjab.

One day Larry and Ashraf were playing together in the church compound while I studied in the adjoining pastoral office. Suddenly I heard a piercing scream of pain and anguish. Rushing outside I saw Larry sitting on a high limb of a tree holding his eye with one hand and holding on to the tree with the other. Ashraf stood below with a homemade bow in his hand and several sharpened sticks on the ground beside him. I took in the picture in a flash and dashed up the tree to grab Larry just as he ceased his screaming. As I carried him to the ground he was trying to explain how the sharp arrow had hit him in the eye and he couldn't see. For some inexplicable reason there seemed to be little pain after the initial impact.

Fearfully, I forced his eyelids apart, and my heart almost stopped beating. A little round red spot of blood in the center of his pupil was slowly enlarging to fill his entire eye. Lu Ann was there by that time, but I did not need her nurse's opinion to know that Larry probably would never see out of his right eye again.

We dashed across the street to our missionary neighbors who had a car, and were on the way to the hospital in a matter of minutes. But it seemed like hours as we waited for the American doctor to see us. Since the eye was filled with blood, it was impossible for him to determine the extent of the injury. Being a general practitioner he was also reluctant to even attempt treatment of the eye. He urged us to take Larry immediately to Dr. Bashir, a Pakistani eye specialist, who headed the eye surgery department of Gunga Ram Hospital. With growing apprehension we drove to his office for another seemingly interminable wait. Dr. Bashir was almost eighty years of age and had spent several years in the United States pursuing his specialty. He inspired confidence and we liked him from the start, but he could not give any prognosis until the blood absorbed from the eye. He was certain there was damage, but could not say how extensive. He did make an appointment for exploratory surgery just a week later to clean out any foreign material that might have remained in the eve. Under general anesthesia, Larry stayed only the one day in the hospital, but he was to wear a bandage for many days as the trauma slowly cleared up.

That uncertain week before surgery was one of agonizing and praying. The other eye seemed to be reacting with some inflammation also, and the doctor had hinted that there could be a serious sympathetic consequence to the uninjured eye. Finally the blood was absorbed and Dr. Bashir was able to make a positive determination that the lens had been destroyed in the eye. He gave us no hope that Larry would ever be able to see more than dark and light from the injured right eye.

For several weeks the danger of infection was present and Dr. Bashir wanted to treat the eye every few days with new medication and dressing. I had bought a used motor bike from a friend, and with Larry behind me, we would zip across town to the doctor's office. Every visit cemented our friendship with Dr. Bashir, and led to long religious discussions about prayer, faith, etc. Although a Mohammedan, Dr. Bashir had many religious doubts concerning his own faith, and I was fascinated to observe how God used Larry's simple testimony to confound the doctor's skepticism.

Even though we trusted the doctor's assurances that nothing at all could be done to restore Larry's vision, we felt that we had to have another specialist confirm the diagnosis. There was some feeling with Lu Ann and me that if we returned to America there might be modern techniques unknown to Dr. Bashir, for saving Larry's sight.

Just at that time a *Reader's Digest* fell into our hands which contained an article entitled, "He Gave Sight to 100,000." It was the dramatic story of Sir Henry Holland, an English eye surgeon who had spent most of his life in Quetta, Pakistan, near the Afghanistan border. He was an old man also, and the article described his outstanding success in saving the sight of thousands who were going blind. Dr. Holland had been knighted by the Queen of England for his meritorious service. During the 1925 earthquake which virtually wiped out the inhabitants of Quetta, Dr. Holland had been the only doctor in that vast territory to minister to the injured.

Quetta was a two-day train trip into the wild tribal territory of the northwest, but I was determined to take Larry to see Sir Henry Holland if he could be contacted. After days of effort, we found out that the good doctor was finishing his last year before retirement to England. We made an appointment by telegram and Larry and I set out on a most interesting train trip into the barren mountain regions bordering the land of Afghanistan.

Dr. Holland received us graciously as guests in his home, and easily qualifies as one of the most outstanding personalities I have ever known. He examined Larry's eye and confirmed what Dr. Bashir had discovered. There was nothing known to medical science that could enable Larry to recover sight in his eye. But Sir Henry spent considerable time convincing us that the loss of an eye would be no great handicap to Larry. He related stories of Lord Nelson and others who excelled in spite of one-eye vision. All in all, it was a most rewarding and reassuring visit, and surely convinced us that we need not cut our mission term short because of Larry's tragic accident.

The reassurances of Dr. Holland have been proven correct by subsequent developments. Larry did adapt easily to the loss of sight in his right eye, and has not allowed the loss to hold him back from all normal functions. Few are able to even detect that the pupil is any different from that of his good left eye.

It was in the middle of the hottest weather, just before the monsoon rains, that I accepted an invitation to Chuharkana Boarding High School as the Week of Prayer speaker. Never have I faced greater handicaps in a preaching series. The school was located in a dry desert area, and the temperatures hovered at the 120-degree mark. I spoke twice a day to a group of students ranging in age from six to twenty-six, and I had to speak through an interpreter.

Any one of those disadvantages would have been discouraging, but I had to hold the attention of that diverse age group, through a slow interpreter, in 120-degree heat. At night we slept on the principal's flat rooftop under a mosquito net, because the inside heat seldom dropped below 100 degrees. The eighteen-inch mud and brick walls simply held the heat of the day and radiated it all night long. I did not envy the American principal of the school who lived his entire five-year term in that desert setting.

As though the forbidding climate was not hostile enough, the next two principals who came to accept that bungalow were shot by bandits. One of them, Dr. Bob Reynolds, was permanently paralyzed by the bullets, and the other one, Mr. Hutchinson, was killed in Bangladesh in 1972 while serving as the principal of another mission high school. Seldom are the dangers and hardships of such service realized until the violence touches one of our own personal friends with its tragedy. In 1971, while holding a series of meetings in Riverside, California, I visited my friend Bob Reynolds in his wheelchair. With incredible courage and perseverance, his brilliant mind forces his hands to painfully peck out articles that counsel other Christian workers. I never failed to be inspired by his courage and determination.

14
Adventures in Moslem Evangelism

From January when we arrived in Pakistan, my primary work was pastoring the large English-speaking church which was located next door to our house. My plans were also laid for a strong evangelistic crusade at the end of the summer. It was very obvious that I would have to change the whole series of sermons to meet the Moslem mentality. The followers of Mohammed were much, much harder to reach with the gospel than the Hindu. In the first place, they were afraid to attend any public Christian meetings for fear of reprisal from relatives. Most of my work for them had to be done in private. Almost daily I talked to fine Moslem young men who were sincerely searching for truth. One group of four came to my office each week for long discussions about Christianity. Two of them were professors at the nearby Islamia College, with graduate degrees in social science. They were not argumentative, and our friendship grew strong and deep during our year of association together.

I shall never forget one prominent Moslem lawyer who made an appointment to see me in my home. He confessed his faith in Christ and his desire to actually become a Christian. After studying the Bible he had decided to contact a Christian pastor to declare his faith. Looking in the phone book he had started at the top of the list of churches. The first pastor he visited was smoking a cigarette and that jolted him considerably. His own Moslem faith forbade the use of tobacco and he decided not to lower his standards to join that Christian church.

The next church he called on had a bingo party in progress and after the pastor defended the practice, he turned away from that one in disappointment. The Moslem religion did not condone gambling and he realized that it would mean lowering his standards to join that church.

The third pastor was a very fundamental Christian who did not believe in either smoking or drinking, but he was skeptical of the lawyer's sincerity. Finally he told the Moslem that he would have to eat some pork in order to prove that he was rejecting his former religion. Of course, the lawyer would not do that because he had discovered that the Bible forbade the use of unclean meat just as the Koran did.

As the lawyer told me about one contact after another with various Christian leaders in Lahore, I was astounded. I knew he was telling the truth because I had studied the Mohammedan holy book, and knew that it did forbid defiling the body with unclean things. And it was true that the personal standards of the Moslem were higher than the Christian churches he had visited. I shall never forget the plea in his voice when he said, "Why should I have to lower my standards in order to become a Christian? I cannot do it."

How glad I was to tell him that there were Christian churches which did not smoke, drink, gamble or eat unclean foods. We spent some enjoyable hours going over other doctrines and truths of the Scriptures which proved to that fine gentleman that true Christianity is much higher than Islam or any other religion in the world. Never in my twenty-five years in the ministry have I heard a sadder commentary on the state of modern Christianity than that lawyer presented. Paul's prophecy about men having only "a form of godliness, but denying the power thereof" was more than fulfilled in the experience he related.

In June as the heat reached toward its peak, 120 degrees, our family packed for the six-week hill leave in the beautiful Himalayan town of Murree. The bus trip was not so enjoyable, but the cool fresh air of the foothills brought new life as we climbed higher to the rest station. A large house had been rented with facilities for four missionary families. An Urdu language teacher had been employed to teach us for about half of each day, and the rest of the time we relaxed and enjoyed each other. Just beyond the range of high mountains lay the fabled Vale of Kashmir with its incomparable beauties, but which we could not visit due to political disputes.

The comforts and conveniences of usual vacation resorts were sadly lacking in our Murree mission house, but it was enough just to be cool and to be with friends. There was no water within a mile of our quarters, so the hired "bishti" made daily climbs to our door with two buckets of water balanced from his shoulder pole. Only after a mysterious fever and diarrhea had struck all of us did we think to check the source of our faithful bishti's water supply. Instead of making the two-mile round trip to a well, he was bringing us water from a nearby polluted stream. Even our boiling was not sufficient to kill those germs!

Near the end of our hill leave I accompanied Neal Sherwin, one of the other missionaries, on a trip to the Khyber Pass. It was a hair-raising trip by bus into a tribal area where every man carries his own law in the form of ax, gun or knife. Winding through the heavily fortified passes of the only northern access route into the country, we came to the last village before entering Afghanistan. Since we could not actually cross the border anyway, we decided to find something to eat and catch the earliest return bus. We were almost starved after the long bus trip, but realized it would be very difficult to find anything to eat in that small military outpost village.

As we walked up and down the streets of the mud-walled village looking for an eating place, a high-ranking military officer suddenly stepped in front of us and saluted. In perfect English he asked if he could help us in any way. We told him that we needed directions to a restaurant. He explained that there was no suitable place for foreign visitors to eat and insisted that we come to his home so that his wife could prepare us food. Delighted to meet such hospitality, we accepted the invitation and soon were relaxing in the comfortable home of this new-found friend. After visiting awhile the officer pulled out two rope cots and urged us to lie down while the food was being prepared. Gratefully we stretched out and, being extremely weary, dropped off to sleep almost immediately. When the food was ready, we were gently awakened to enjoy one of the most delicious meals I had ever eaten. The officer would not consider accepting any payment for the food, and we went on our way amazed at the unusual display of "Christian" concern for others.

Of course, the man was not a Christian at all; he was a Mohammedan. But his kind hospitality went far beyond the way most American Christians practice the Sermon on the Mount. I often thought about the tremendous zeal of the Moslems for practicing their religion. If only they would accept the Saviour as more than a great prophet! They are not afraid to stand firmly for what they believe. I've seen Moslem men spread their prayer rugs on a crowded bus seat, and kneel awkwardly for ten minutes on the swaying seat, facing what they hoped was Mecca. When the time comes to pray, they are not embarrassed to pray, no matter who is watching. Something must be said for that kind of fervor and moral courage. I'm afraid the average Christian doesn't even think of praying five times a day, let alone actually do it where someone might see. This is one reason a converted Moslem makes a strong Christian; it costs him something to become one, and he doesn't give it up easily.

When we returned to Lahore the intense dry heat was giving way to the extreme humidity of the monsoon season. It was hard to know which was more miserable, but we knew things would be better as soon as the rains were over. I had plans all laid for a big public evangelistic crusade during that early autumn period when the weather was absolutely perfect. We secured the Burt Railroad Institute for the meetings, a very prestigious auditorium in Lahore. It was a good series, but we knew there had been no breakthrough at all into the hardcore Moslem community. How we longed for some way to bring them to a public confession of Christ! I talked to scores of them who were "secret disciples" of Jesus. They dared not risk their lives by any type of public acknowledgment, because their own relatives would consider it a duty to kill them.

Only rarely did we find Mohammedans who had the faith and courage to take an open stand for Christ. But one of them was Saddiq, whom I'd like to tell you about right now. I first met this unusual man on Christmas day, 1956, soon after our Burt Institute meetings were ended. He knocked at my door and asked if I would baptize him that very day. He had attended the evangelistic tent meetings of a fellow missionary in the city of Peshawar further to the north. Night after night he listened to the sermons from outside the tent where no one could see his interest. Finally he knew there was nothing else to do but follow Christ all the way.

After making his decision to be a Christian, Saddiq announced to his wife that he was going to be baptized.

The next day he returned home to find his house empty. His wife and children had been taken away by his father-in-law, and so had all the furniture as well. He was never to see his family again.

A few days later he lost his good job with the government because his relatives intervened against him. And soon after that he was waylaid by some of his relatives and beaten almost to death. Although left for dead, he managed to survive and escape. Fleeing as a refugee from his own family he came to the teeming city of Lahore to seek safety and to be baptized.

Examination proved that Saddiq was ready for baptism. He was not only fully surrendered to Christ but he understood the Bible reasons for his faith. Since he had no personal friends in Lahore and since he wanted to seal his decision without further delay, I filled the chapel baptistry immediately. A few of the missionary family members came in for the brief baptismal service. I will not soon forget that baptism. Saddiq's face was lined with scars which he will bear the rest of his life from that terrible beating. When he entered the water that day he was leaving everything for Christ—his home, family, job and almost his own life. He would have to hide out as a fugitive from his relatives for the rest of his life, and never be permitted to see his wife or children again! Any relative who found him would consider it a duty to kill him.

Saddiq became a faithful member of my church and we provided a room for him behind the mission headquarters building. He secured work representing the interests of our student cereal industry of the boarding high school at Chuharkana. But one day he came to my office with a burden. He pleaded that the mission send him into Afghanistan to distribute Christian literature. He would go as a cloth salesman and give away the Word of God to those who were interested.

Of course it was an impossible request because no Christians were permitted in Afghanistan. He would be killed within days of undertaking such a venture. But Saddiq begged us to let him run the risk. Since he had given up everything else for his Saviour he was not afraid to lay down his life also.

I've probably thought of Saddiq a thousand times since returning to America—usually while holding evangelistic crusades. When I listen to people making excuses for not going all the way with Jesus, I think of Saddiq. When men hold back from keeping the Sabbath for fear of losing their jobs, I think of Saddiq. When I see the men and women who do not have the courage or faith to inconvenience themselves for the truth's sake, I think of Saddiq. And then I realize that we don't really sacrifice anything for Christ's sake.

I've seen elegant women who wouldn't be baptized because it would mean surrendering some of their vain attire. One young girl was not willing to give up her dancing for Christ. Few Christians today understand at all what Jesus meant when He said, "Whosoever he be of you that forsaketh not all that he hath, he cannot be my disciple" (Luke 14:33). "If any man will come after me, let him deny himself, and take up his cross daily, and follow me" (Luke 9:23). No wonder Jesus said, "... and few there be that find it" (Matt. 7:14). The majority of people are looking for a smooth, comfortable, easy religion. They do not love Christ enough to give up anything for Him. The Master's doctrine of self-denial is totally unknown to them.

15
From Karachi to Texas

As the time approached for our furlough, the excitement increased in proportion. It had been almost five years since we had seen our loved ones. For weeks we made plans, drew up an itinerary of travel schedules, and sold belongings that were not needed. In fact, we had decided to take nothing back to America except my books and our suitcases of clothes and personal effects.

Our plans included two months of travel through the Middle East and Europe, so there were visas and travel permits to arrange. Finally the last items were sold, the tickets were in hand, and we took the train to Karachi for the last few days of settling departure red tape. It was the first week of April when we boarded a plane in Karachi for the first lap of our homeward journey.

It would require a full volume to tell all the interesting details of two weeks with Mary and Bob seeing the Holy Land. Bob spoke fluent Arabic and took us to the most interesting sights. By that time they had been forced out of Amman, Jordan, by political unrest and were living in Beirut, Lebanon.

Because of the Suez Canal closing and deterioration of relations between America and Egypt, no United States citizens were permitted in Egypt. But the day before leaving Beirut we received word that the restrictions had been lifted, so we quickly booked a reservation to Cairo. There we spent three wonderful days seeing the pyramids and taking an overnight run to Luxor to visit the Valley of the Kings.

Flying on to Athens we spent Sabbath with a group of Christian young people on Mars Hill, singing choruses and sharing our testimony with them. Then on to Rome where we took a train for our leisurely trip northward through Switzerland, Germany, Holland, France and England. It was a glorious experience and we regretted that the children were not old enough to remember the historic places for later educational reference.

The final lap of travel was made by ship from England to New York on the Queen Elizabeth. What a contrast to the slow freighter which had carried us away from America just five years earlier! As we spent our last night at sea there was little sleeping for Lu Ann and me. We could scarcely contain our excitement as we looked forward to the next day when Lu Ann's folks would meet us at the New York landing. We wondered how much they had changed during those five years.

How can one describe the thrill of seeing that majestic Statue of Liberty after five years? And then we could see the throngs of people on the pier as the great liner drew near to dock. We strained to see the familiar faces. The emotional tension was enormous, and there were tears of joy as we embraced those dear ones after so long a separation.

I have often looked back upon that poignant moment and the tumultuous reunion. It was too wonderful to describe. Yet it was nothing compared to the great homecoming we shall experience when Jesus comes. Then we shall see loved ones who have been separated from us by the hand of death, and there will be no shadow of fear or dread for the future. We shall not wonder how the infirmities of old age have affected our loved ones, because immortal youth will erase all possibility of pain or illness.

Our first month back home was spent with our parents letting them get acquainted with the grandson they had never seen. At the same time we were in contact with our Mission Board as they tried to secure a visa for an entrance into Burma or Ceylon. There were calls for evangelists in both Rangoon and Colombo, but the countries were not permitting new foreign mission workers to come in on any basis. We would have welcomed either spot because it would have involved continued public evangelism. In Pakistan there was no scope for reaching the Moslem in a public way, so we had decided not to return there. Finally we received a letter regretfully advising that no visas were forthcoming and we should accept our return to the States as permanent.

Within hours of receiving that news from the Mission Board, a telephone call came through from Pastor Robert Pierson in Texas, asking me to accept a church in Austin, the state capital. He invited me to fly there immediately to look over the housing possibilities and to confer with the departing pastor. When I arrived in Austin, it was immediately obvious that we would have an educational problem. The church school was very small and limited in grades and staffing. Both our older sons had received their early teaching from Lu Ann and now needed an expert educator to determine where they belonged in a graded system.

When I pointed out the problem to Pastor Pierson, the president of the Texas Conference, he readily agreed that Austin would not be the best place for our children. He was also an India missionary veteran and understood some of the problems we faced in this area. So he asked us to go to Dallas and pastor the Oak Cliff church on a temporary basis until another anticipated church opening developed.

I speak of this Austin incident only because it ties in with a tragic drama which unfolded during the next twelve months while serving the Oak Cliff congregation. At the time we did not understand why the first call to Austin closed up to us. Later we understood clearly that God had a hand in it. He was leading us to Dallas for a very unusual and important reason which I would like to share with you now.

It is not easy to speak of this experience. I force myself to draw upon some painful memories only because it will demonstrate the tremendous way God leads in the salvation of souls.

For several days our family lived in a Dallas motel while we searched for a house to rent in the Oak Cliff area. On the second evening in the motel it suddenly occurred to me that an old college friend, David Hale, lived in the city of Dallas. I had first met Dave in 1945 at Southern Missionary College when he was a freshman and I was a junior. As a monitor in the boys' dormitory, I would chat with Dave as he passed my desk in the hallway. He was extremely likeable and seemed to appreciate the fact that I took a special interest in him. As a ministerial student I looked for opportunities to encourage some of the younger boys in the dormitory, and I could see that Dave was associating with a group of friends who were not helping him at all.

I found opportunity to speak to Dave about his friends and instead of resenting it, he responded very favorably. Even though he was a pre-medical student, there was a tie of mutual friendship which existed between us. Later in the year he left the college to continue his studies elsewhere, and I lost track of him. In fact, it was almost exactly ten years later, while living in Bangalore, India, that I received an unexpected letter from Dave postmarked in Dallas, Texas. Somewhere he had read a report of my work in India, and had gotten hold of my address. In the letter he mentioned how he still remembered the good talks we had in college, and just wanted to renew the contact. Several letters went back and forth. I questioned him about his religious faith, but he always scrupulously skirted the matter in his letters to me. He was taking a medical residency in Dallas, had two little boys, and a wonderful wife named Betty whom I had never met. But there was no mention of church or religion. It seemed strange that he would write to me after so many years, especially when he seemed to have no particular interest in religion.

There had been no letters for a few weeks and we left India for Pakistan. Then we were back home and searching for a house in Dallas. That's when I remembered Dave again, and grabbed the motel phone book to look up his number. His wife Betty answered the phone, and she remembered my name as Dave's friend and promised to tell him as soon as he came in.

Within an hour Dave bounced up the steps of the motel room and knocked at the door. What a joy it was to see him again after twelve years! And he seemed just as glad to see me. It was very apparent that Dave was not very close to the church any more. But he seemed delighted to learn that I was to be living in Dallas and wanted to know where the church was located. Then we learned the amazing fact that he only lived a few blocks from my church.

On the basis of our friendship, Dave and Betty began to attend my wonderful little church and I started a regular Tuesday night Bible study in their home every week. It was a rewarding experience to see their faith grow week by week. Finally, we finished all the scheduled series of lessons and Betty made her decision to accept Christ fully into her life and be baptized. Dave had been baptized years before, but he made a new commitment of his life to follow Christ fully.

What a day it was when the Oak Cliff church received the Hale family into its fellowship! During those months of study Dave had become one of my closest friends. He and his family had also been drawn into the warm fellowship of the Young Married Couples' Club of the church.

Within two or three weeks of the baptism, the Barron Brothers Evangelistic Team came to Oak Cliff for a two week series of tent meetings. Dave and Betty were right in the middle of the plans and preparation. Both served as ushers and greeters at the large tent which stood on a prominent corner of Zangs Boulevard.

During the crusade Dave's parents came down to visit from Louisville, Kentucky, and I met them for the first time. They were dedicated Christian folks and it was a pleasure to get acquainted with them. They had special reasons to rejoice as they watched Dave function in the meetings as a strong witnessing Christian. They had to leave before the series was over, but I have every reason to believe that God brought them there to give them assurance that Dave was fully committed to the Lord Jesus. They needed that assurance a few days later and God had prepared them for it.

The last night of the tent meetings was a busy occasion. Many decisions had been made for Christ, and they had to be instructed in the after-class. Then it was announced that volunteers were needed to help take down the tent that very night. A few laymen stayed to work with the ministers in dismantling the four-pole tent for removal to the next crusade site.

Dave was among those who stayed to help. He and I worked together most of the time that evening and it was long after midnight when the canvas was safely stowed away, and we approached the final job of lowering the steel poles. Two were safely on the ground and Dave, Henry Barron and I were kneeling together to pull the two sections of the poles apart. Suddenly we heard a shout. I looked up in time to glimpse a falling pole, but there was no time to move from my tracks. It fell into the midst of our little cluster, barely missing Henry and me, but striking Dave on the head and shoulder. He fell without making a sound and it is certain he never realized what struck him.

While the ambulance was being called, we knelt by Dave feeling all the agonizing frustration and remorse that overwhelms one in such a moment. I rode in the screaming ambulance to the emergency room, but I think all of us knew that it was too late for help. I remember standing by as the doctor massaged his chest and then turned with a hopeless gesture. Then I recall rushing into an empty room to lean against the wall weeping. There's where one of the ministers found me who had driven my car behind the ambulance.

Then the numbing realization slowly came to me that I must go to Betty and break the news to her. I knew Lu Ann would have to be with me for that terrible task, so we drove to the parsonage to pick her up. Never have I dreaded anything as much as I dreaded that responsibility. Betty was so close to Dave and leaned on him so much, I could hardly think of waking her up with this news. What a test for a newborn Christian to face only days after her baptism!

Just before leaving the parsonage I called the hospital where Dave was affiliated and talked to a shocked colleague who promised to meet me at Betty's as soon as possible. A few minutes after we had given her the message, the doctor and his wife arrived. It was just as terrible as we had feared it would be for Betty. We did not leave her until the next afternoon when two private planes arrived from Louisville, supplied by Dave's cousin who owned a charter plane service. One of them took Betty and the children and in the other one I accompanied Dave's body back to Louisville. During the night I had talked to the parents on the phone, and they had asked me to take the funeral service if I could.

It was one of the most painful funerals I have ever conducted, but how comforting it was to know that Dave was ready for that tragic experience. For Betty it was too shocking to comprehend. Months would pass by before she could sort out the lines of God's overruling providence and love. But she weathered the storm and her faith was built back through years of severe test and trauma.

Because we had been such close friends, after Dave's death the elder Hales drew me into their family and became like second parents to me. As I stood by them in the Evergreen Cemetery in Louisville, speaking words of comfort over Dave's casket, I had no way of knowing that in just a few years my own youngest son would be laid to rest only several feet away from Dave's grave. And incredible as it may seem, Mrs. Hale was standing by Ronnie's side when he breathed his last just as I had stood by her son at the end. But that is another heartbreaking story that will come later if I can find the strength to share it with you.

Within a few days of Dave's funeral I was transferred from Dallas to another church in San Antonio, Texas. Only then did all the events of the past year start fitting into a pattern. I began to understand why the Austin church did not work out. God sent me to Dallas to help Dave get ready for the tragedy which was ahead. Perhaps no one could have reached him at the time except me. Because of our past friendship it was possible to accomplish in that year exactly what was needed to restore Dave spiritually and prepare Betty for the future. I stayed in Dallas just long enough to see that experience through and then was transferred. How strange and inexplicable are God's ways, and only in the Kingdom will we find all the answers to our questions.

In San Antonio, besides shepherding a lovely congregation of four hundred, I had the privilege of ministering to two hundred young servicemen each week who also worshiped in my church. It was while I served there in 1959, that my father passed away at the age of 81 years. I was able to be by his side when he breathed his last after a coma of several days' duration. The greatest assurance of all was that he died in the faith. He was ready to go.

God gave us much wonderful fruit in San Antonio in the two ten-week tent crusades which were conducted. Space would not permit a recital of individual victories scored by those who came up the sawdust aisle to accept Christ fully. One young soldier gave his heart to the Lord and was baptized. Shortly afterward he was transferred and I did not hear from him anymore. Then just thirteen years later, as I conducted a one-week camp meeting series near Columbus, Ohio, I met that soldier boy again. He was on the grounds to represent a Christian sales company that manufactured Bible School material. As we visited together, Ross told me that he was the first member of his family to become a Christian, but that over thirty of his relatives or in-laws had been baptized in the last thirteen years as a result of his testimony!

While serving as the pastor in San Antonio, I baptized another young soldier, little realizing that he would later play a large role in my future ministry. Wayne Coulter, at this writing, is the chairman of the Amazing Facts Board of Directors. As a pastor, evangelist, conference president and chairman of our board, he has been a stalwart defender of truth through the years. How little we can see of the endless chain of prayer and power which links with one soul who goes all the way with Christ!

16
Brain Tumor! Test of Faith

My next assignment was in Fort Worth, Texas, where I had the joy of building a beautiful new sanctuary for one of the finest congregations I've ever been privileged to pastor. Again we were busily occupied with public evangelism. It was while serving in that historic old "cow town" of the West that we faced the most severe test of our lives.

That nineteen-month Gethsemane began for us when seven-year-old Ronnie, our youngest, began to complain of a headache and nausea. Always the picture of health, we had no reason to feel that he could have anything more than an uncomfortable siege of cold or flu misery. On the third day of his symptoms I casually mentioned them to Dr. Skinner, one of the three fine doctors who served as officers of my church. He was instantly alert and said he wanted to come by the parsonage immediately to see him.

After a few perfunctory tests, Dr. Skinner asked us to bring Ronnie to the hospital for a spinal tap because there was some indication of pressure on the brain. We took him that very same afternoon and Dr. Skinner had arranged for a specialist to be present for the procedure. The results were conclusive that there was a growth of some sort, probably a brain tumor, creating pressure on the spinal fluid. I think it was almost as hard for my dear doctor friend to give us the report as it was for us to receive it.

The next step was to locate a neurosurgeon who would perform further tests and probably surgery. We investigated several names and made a number of long distance telephone calls to check out neurosurgeons in the Dallas-Fort Worth area to whom we might commit the life of our son. We have always felt that God directed us in choosing Dr. Ronald Smith of Fort Worth, a man who gave us comfort along with a tremendous degree of skill and competency.

Dr. Smith spent quite a bit of time explaining that there was about a 50-50 chance of the tumor being nonmalignant. Only the actual operation could give verification of that crucial question. He explained that a myelogram test just prior to the surgery would give a final confirmation of the existence and location of the growth. While Ronnie was still asleep, following the myelogram, they would proceed with the operation.

There is no way to describe the emotional suspense of those few days of waiting. Lu Ann and I were in prayer most of the time over the impending surgery. We found it almost impossible to believe that our buoyant, exuberant little boy had become one of the unlikely statistics of child brain tumors. In fact, the initial symptoms disappeared during the week following the spinal tap. That was the week Ronnie had further extended tests in the hospital. How we prayed that the preliminary myelogram would reveal no growth at all! Yet we offered our prayers always according to God's will for his life.

The five-hour operation was performed at St. Joseph's Hospital in Fort Worth. Dr. Gerald King, another faithful member of my church, had volunteered to assist in the delicate surgery. Lu Ann and I spent those hours in much heart-searching and prayer. As a minister, I had no pastor to whom I could turn, yet we knew that our five hundred church members were holding us up to God in their prayers. One of my closest associates, Pastor Bill May, came by the hospital during the operation and stayed with us until the doctors had emerged with their report. No one will ever know how much it meant to have that trusted friend to just sit with us in sympathy and concern.

The exhausted doctors could only tell us that the tumor was large and that it was located in the cerebellum, one of the most delicate areas of the brain where most of the vital functions are centralized. They had tried to remove it all, but could not be sure because of the sensitivity of the area. In fact, they could not even be certain that the brain had not been bruised during the operation, in which case death could follow within twenty-four hours when the brain would begin to swell. At least he had survived the surgery. One out of ten patients did not live through that particular type of operation. They would not know whether it was malignant for two or three more days, after exhaustive laboratory examination.

For the next several hours Lu Ann did not leave his side in the intensive care unit. As a registered nurse, she was permitted to stay with him, and much of the time I was there also, watching Ronnie struggle through those agonizingly slow faltering breaths, every one of which threatened to be his last. Then, suddenly, he was awake, talking and moving his arms and the doctors were delighted, just as we were. Only then did Dr. King tell us about the surgery. At the most crucial point in the excision of the tumor, the tissues began to bleed excessively. It was impossible to even touch the brain with a piece of cotton and there was no way to proceed. It seemed that the entire operation was going to be in vain. Just at that moment, when many doctors would have cursed in frustration, Dr. Smith lowered his hands and prayed aloud, "Oh God, help me." With awe in his voice, Dr. King told us how almost instantly the blood stopped flowing, and Dr. Smith quietly proceeded with the infinitely tedious operation.

Two days later the laboratory report brought the dismal news that the brain tumor had been one of the most malignant types, medulla blastoma. Dr. Smith kindly explained to us that there was no medical hope for Ronnie to survive that particular type of brain tumor. In answer to our anxious questions he estimated no more than two years at the most that we would have our little boy with us. He could make no prognosis about the developing course of the cancer, or what physical complications we could expect. Every case was different, depending on the cranial nerves affected by the tumor.

The operation took place in March, 1962, and Ronnie made an exceptionally fine recovery from the massive ordeal. By September he was chafing to enter school, and there seemed to be no reason at all why he could not proceed full speed ahead. He was reading almost as well as Dennis and Larry, and had an amazing capacity for absorbing knowledge. How excited he was to begin that first year of study in a classroom! But within six weeks he began to complain of a pain in his spine. Rapidly the pain increased in intensity and we hurried back to Dr. Smith.

He informed us that radiation was the only recourse open to relieve the obviously metastasized tumor cells now rapidly reproducing in his spine. Thus began the long series of visits to the radiation center under the direction of gentle Dr. Morphis, another man we came to appreciate very deeply. Almost as soon as one area of back or head was irradiated, the pain would appear in another spot—series after series—until finally he had received the maximum allowed, some ninety treatments in all. Fortunately, there were no miserable side effects except the loss of hair, and there was almost immediate relief in every series of radiation except one. In that instance they were inadvertently missing the localized cancer spot, and the growth quickly immobilized Ronnie with excruciating pain and partial paralysis in the legs. From that paralysis he never fully recovered.

The last four months of his life were months of constant pain. Sometimes Lu Ann would have to give him twenty shots in one day. Fortunately, we were able to keep him at home since the doctors could do no more for his relief. But in spite of the suffering, Ronnie was one of the bravest little Christians to the very end of his life. He did not complain. Once he asked his mother to write down a list of things he was thankful for. I still cherish that list that a dying little boy could tabulate. At the last he did not want stories read to him—only the Bible. One day, after hours of terrible pain, he burst into singing that rang through the house:

"Trust and obey,
For there's no other way
To be happy in Jesus,
But to trust and obey."

Members of our church in Fort Worth surrounded us with their love and assistance. For weeks the ladies brought food for all of us while Lu Ann was spending full time at Ronnie's side. No one could have done more for their pastor than those wonderful people.

Our two older boys, Larry and Dennis, suffered silently as they could see their little brother growing more and more ill. They helped in many, many ways around the house, as they had learned from their earliest years. They also assisted, as they were able, in Ronnie's care—entertaining him when he would feel better, bringing him juices to help fulfill his fluid intake quota, helping change his bed, etc.

Two months before Ronnie's death, after consultation with the doctors and much prayer, I accepted a call to pastor a large church in Louisville, Kentucky. Miraculously, Ronnie made the move with a minimum of difficulty, even though we stopped in a motel overnight on the way. Another tremendous congregation was waiting to take us to their hearts in Louisville, including Dave Hale's father and mother.

It would be impossible to bare my heart to anyone concerning those last days of Ronnie's life. Lu Ann had the hardest part to bear in constant attention and increasing ministry to Ronnie's every need. I could not have endured what she had to bear—suffering with him in every pain. Sometimes I would fall on my face in my church office and pray and weep. Everything had been done that we knew to do—prayers, anointing, commitment. We felt that we would gladly suffer and die in Ronnie's place if it were possible. We could not understand God's purpose in allowing him to suffer, yet we never questioned God's love and providence. We knew Satan had caused the cancer, but God had seen fit to allow it. Now He wanted us to really believe that promise that "all things work together for good to them that love God" (Rom. 8:28). For years I had comforted the bereaved with the promises of God's Word, and had assured them that God was able to sustain them. Now I had to prove that those assurances were not just empty words. Not one of them failed.

A few hours before he died on October 25, 1963, Ronnie's mind was just as keen as it ever had been, in spite of medication for pain. Then he seemed to slip into a restless coma, although he could still hold up his finger when I asked him to. Shortly he became paralyzed from the waist down, and then his arms ceased their thrashing about. Later that night his breathing became more and more shallow until it ceased entirely.

It was a terrible experience to watch our little boy's life slip away, but we also were comforted to know that the suffering was over. Our greatest comfort of all was to know that Ronnie would be sleeping until the glorious resurrection morning when we would see him again. Jesus taught that death is a sleep, and for Ronnie it will only seem a moment before he awakens to see Jesus coming in clouds of glory. What a reunion day that will be, and how I long to take my little boy in my arms again. What an incentive to be faithful so that I can meet my blessed Saviour, and also my fully restored son.

One of those who stood by our side when Ronnie breathed his last was Mrs. Hale, who had come to spend the night and give Lu Ann some needed relief. How strange that just five years earlier I had stood by her son, Dave, as he also went to sleep in Christ. Ronnie was laid to rest in Evergreen Cemetery just a few feet from Dave's resting place. Three years later I returned to that same cemetery to conduct the funeral for Dave's father who was buried near Ronnie and Dave. As I gazed again upon those hallowed spots my mind went forward to the day when death, the last great enemy, will be eternally broken and destroyed.

17
Preachers in Doubt

Two and a half years of pastoral evangelism in Louisville, Kentucky, brought a most heartening result. The church was tuned to soulwinning and strong lay leaders made it a perfect joy to conduct public decision crusades. During those years also I had the opportunity to see firsthand some of the fearful fruits of modernism and theological skepticism. For years I had read the incredible reports of liberal professors in the seminaries who did not really believe the Word of God. Often I would dismiss the stories as absurd fabrications written, no doubt, by some wild-eyed evangelist type. Surely no man of the cloth could doubt the great fundamental scriptural doctrines of inspiration, divine creation, the resurrection, miracles and the second coming of Jesus. But I was to learn that the situation was even more terrible in those theological centers than the magazine articles had portrayed it.

After lecturing in the two largest Protestant seminaries in Louisville, I was approached by the student officers of one of them to take part in a very formal symposium discussion on the topic of the second advent of Jesus. The symposium was sponsored by the Cultural Affairs and Social Action Committee of the Louisville Presbyterian Theological Seminary. I was asked to present the pre-millennial view of the coming of Jesus, while Dr. George Edwards, professor of New Testament theology took the post-millennial view, and Dr. Ulrich Mauser, Biblical theology professor, stood somewhere in between. Invitations went out to ministers and theological students of the city, and the chapel was packed to the aisles on November 20, 1964. It was obvious that there was an unusual interest in this topic.

Since I was the visiting member of the panel I was given the choice of when to speak. Each of us had about fifteen minutes to present our material and then the meeting would open to questions from the floor. I chose to speak last. Dr. Mauser, a German theologian, spoke first, and he had his ten points carefully written out word for word. Amazingly he did not make a single slight reference to the Bible. But he did make this verbatim remark on one of his ten propositions: "Anyone who believes that he knows the slightest thing about the second coming of Jesus is stupid and sacrilegious."

Dr. Edwards was an eloquent, bombastic man who spoke without notes, and he made reference to only one Bible text during his discourse. Near the end of his talk he astounded the audience with this statement: "I do not believe in the second coming of Jesus. We do not teach it in this institution. I have been a professor in this seminary for nine years and this chapel has never heard a sermon on the second coming of Jesus."

I was almost too amazed to get up and speak. It seemed impossible that I had heard the two theologians correctly. For days I had prepared to answer any theoretical fancies and interpretations about the advent, but I was totally unprepared to have the doctrine denied and tossed out the window. After all, there are 331 references to His coming in the 260 chapters of the New Testament alone. What I had heard sounded absolutely insane coming from teachers of the Word. I remember that my first words were, "On the basis of what Dr. Edwards has said, this chapel is about to hear its first sermon on the second advent of Christ." And in the next fifteen minutes I gave twenty-two texts on that beautiful doctrine.

The reaction was overwhelming. One after another of the students jumped to his feet to ask further questions about the Bible and its message. For one hour I stood at the desk explaining and building the case stronger with each answer. Finally, Dr. Edwards could stand it no longer. He leaped to his feet, red-faced, and fairly screamed at the audience, "Students, please! The very idea that Christ is going to come floating down on a white cloud to bail us out of the trouble we got ourselves into!" Then he began to ridicule the thrilling doctrine of Christ's second coming. Slowly an old man arose in the audience—a professor at the Presbyterian Seminary, I learned later—and said, "It is true that we do not teach this subject anymore in this seminary, but we have to admit that what Mr. Crews has said today is exactly what the early church taught. It bothers me that we do not teach it anymore." And he sat down.

After the dismissal students crowded around me for another hour asking more questions and hungrily drinking in the Bible answers. When I asked their thinking on subjects such as the resurrection, they said, "We don't know what we believe on these things because our professors don't know what they believe." I felt so sorry for those young men who were soon to be graduating and pastoring churches, yet did not believe the Bible. They did not even know what the Bible taught. *Redbook* magazine surely was correct in reporting the results of a survey in the eight leading seminaries of America. They found that only one percent of the students in those seminaries believed in the second advent of Christ. What a tragedy of modern disbelief and skepticism!

18
Ventures in Radio

Early in 1965 a telephone call from Baltimore, Maryland, placed me in contact again with my friend from Texas days, Bill May. As evangelism secretary of the Chesapeake Conference, he was exploring the idea of a daily radio broadcast which could reach millions of materialistic Americans with the Bible message. Plans and format were still indefinite, but he wanted me to join him and Cyril Miller, whom I had also known in the Southwest, in developing a saturation radio plan to cover the states of Maryland and Delaware. They also wanted me to be the broadcast speaker.

Although the sketchy outline sounded reasonable and appealing on the telephone, I was totally unconvinced that I could be a successful radio speaker. In all my life I had only spoken two or three times over the air, and had no illusions at all that I could become an effective broadcaster. Therefore, I rejected the invitation and pondered only briefly why those two visionary friends of mine had such a strange conviction about my being a radio preacher.

I soon forgot about the conversation, but two months later, one midnight, I was jangled awake by the telephone to find Bill May on the other end of the line again. Subsequent years of close association would reveal that Bill May often worked while other men slept. As a veritable dynamo of ideas and action, he has been the most thoroughly organized and the most effective leader of men I have ever known.

In that second conversation, Bill went into more detail

to describe the exciting new series of color folders he was preparing as a Bible course for the daily radio broadcast. Somehow his enthusiasm and persuasion came through the phone to convince me that they were moving into an area of soulwinning that could not help but succeed. He told me about the prayers and the preliminary plans that had already gone into the project. By the end of that extended midnight phone conversation, I also was excited about the challenge of a refreshing new approach to reaching a secular radio audience with the truth of God. I promised Bill that I would pray about it and let him know shortly.

Within the next few days some unusual circumstances developed in relation to my ministry which seemed to point in the direction of accepting the call. Much prayer also brought increasing conviction that God wanted us to join the new experimental radio work in Baltimore. We dreaded the thought of leaving such a devoted and dedicated congregation who had stood so close to us in our bereavement over Ronnie, but we felt that God had opened the door.

In October we moved to the Baltimore area and began to lay plans for launching the broadcast. Cyril, Bill and I spent weeks brainstorming the ideas, and hammering out details of the plan. Since Bill had already authored the first of the ten full-color Information Folders, and had given them the title, "Amazing Facts," we decided to call the broadcast by that name also. While he moved into a crash program of completing the series of folders, I set up a deadline schedule for preparing radio scripts.

I was overwhelmed by the thought of getting those hundreds of broadcast messages ready for our launching date. I felt that it was almost necessary to have a six months' supply on hand at the time we started airing the program. In the meantime, the basic philosophy of our radio approach began to crystallize in our committee discussions. We agreed the broadcast should be fifteen minutes in length, that it should have a secular news commentary approach; and that it should focus on giving the full doctrinal message of the Bible in a direct, forthright manner. Our burden was for those million people who would instantly turn to another station if a religious song or prayer came over the air. In order to capture their interest or curiosity, to keep them listening, I decided to research some of the most amazing facts in history and use them to catch the ear of the nonreligious listeners as well as the Christian audience. Later I was convinced that God had led in that decision, because a number of radio stations changed their policies which had been against airing daily religion, because of the secular news flavor of our program introduction.

We secured initial contracts with three fine stations in Maryland which fairly well covered the two-state Chesapeake area. WBMD in Baltimore was the first one to air "Amazing Facts" beginning in June of 1966. After almost twenty years at the radio 750 spot on the dial, hundreds of letters continue to pour in from listeners on that popular station. I shall never forget the circumstances leading up to the first soul who was baptized as a result of the broadcast. He was Floyd Miller, a young man who worked as a car salesman in Essex, Maryland. He heard the very first program on WBMD and seldom missed after that. Letters full of questions flowed in from Floyd, then a telephone call, and finally a personal visit. It cost him something to make his decision to follow Christ all the way. He met opposition and persecution within his own family, but moved out anyway to put Christ uppermost in his life. Friends told him he would starve to death if he kept the true Bible Sabbath because Saturday was the busiest day in the car-selling business. Floyd claimed the promises of God and stepped out into the waters of baptism. The year following his baptism, in spite of keeping the Sabbath (or I should say because of his Sabbathkeeping) Floyd made 50 percent more money than he had the year before. What a testimony to the power of God's blessing! Later Floyd served with distinction for seven years as the manager of the Amazing Facts' ministries. Thousands of others all over North America can trace their introduction to Christ and His message back to the Amazing Facts broadcast and its prodigious literature outreach.

By the end of 1985 over forty books had been published by Amazing Facts, many of them on subjects long neglected or misunderstood. The doctrinal series of twenty-six booklets entitled "Library of Sermons" has proven to be the most popular material produced for the ministry.

In 1980, Amazing Facts ventured into television with a five minute daily telecast on a Hagerstown cable station. Later, that series of 210 programs was updated and reproduced with the latest technology, and introduced via satellite network to a potential audience of twenty million viewers all across the United States.

In 1984, two important steps were taken to broaden the influence of the mushrooming ministry. A health evangelist joined the evangelistic teams to effect an inspired union of health and religion. At the same time all phases of our soulwinning program, including the public crusades, were videotaped in their live, platform format to be made available at an economical cost. Today the evangelistic series, *Healthline* series, and cooking school series are all popular parts of the total Amazing Facts package available for individuals and/or churches to use in their witnessing projects.

The headquarters of the Amazing Facts ministry is

now located in Frederick, Maryland, a one-hour drive west from its original administrative home in Columbia, Maryland. The details of that providential development constitutes another one of the incredible stories so characteristic of this miracle ministry.

For years we operated out of three rooms in the basement of the Chesapeake Conference office in Columbia. The crowded conditions allowed for no growth and the frustrations multiplied with the increasing requirements for space and personnel. Although we advertised for other facilities, not one suitable suggestion came to us. Under that restricted arrangement we had not been able to save a penny of money for any capital improvement. In my perplexity and concern I decided to devote a full day to prayer and fasting over the matter of our pressing office needs. It was obvious that no further expansion of our ministry was possible unless we could find more commodious quarters.

From that experience I have learned not to ask God for something unless I am prepared for the answer. I had faith that doors would begin to open for us, but I must confess that I didn't expect things to move as swiftly as they did. Let me share with you the mind-boggling events which followed each other over the next few days after my Sabbath of special prayer. Please keep in mind that all of these things occurred within a week or so.

Dr. Frank Damazo, a prominent surgeon in Frederick, and a personal friend, called me and offered to give Amazing Facts an acre of land adjacent to the Interstate 70 highway in Frederick. That gift of real estate was later appraised at $54,500. I accepted it gratefully. The next day I received a telephone call from Mr. G. G. Welch, a retired businessman in North Carolina, who had been a faithful supporter of Amazing Facts from its inception. In the course of the conversation I mentioned the acre of land which had been given the day before. Mr. Welch reacted with unexpected enthusiasm. "I'd like to come up and see the land," he said, "My wife and I will drive up this week and look at it."

Even though he was over 80 years of age, Mr. Welch walked over that beautiful level ground with obvious excitement. Standing in the middle of it he said, "If you build your office here, I will give you $30,000 to get started."

From that point the momentum never let up. The day after Mr. Welch's visit my brother dropped by to visit me from Florida. Before leaving he handed me a check for $10,000 to apply on the building. Later that week Jerry Mayes arrived as the new treasurer of Amazing Facts. For years he had been a building contractor, and when he heard all that had happened in one week, he said, "Let's start putting up the building. We have enough in hand to do a lot of the work."

These were dizzying developments! We drew some fast plans, called for volunteer helpers, and set a work day. The results? Ninety days later the 8,000 sq. ft. building was finished, furnished, and all of it paid for! After years of trying to find a new location, and with no money on hand to even make a beginning, God took us, in just three months, from nothing to a beautiful debt-free center worth at least $300,000.

This train of events taught me that this Amazing Facts ministry is God's program. It has been called to a unique witness in these times of compromise and conformity. I have suffered a tremendous sense of inadequacy in meeting the demands of preaching, writing and administration. Yet God has never relieved me of the burden to proclaim the strong, straight message of reformation truths which have been so greatly diluted and watered-down in these Laodicean days. If there has been uncertainty in any area, it has not been over the type of bold, revivalistic ministry which has been assigned to this special organization. It is a conviction which permeates the thinking of every employee, evangelist and board member of Amazing Facts. We feel that the blessing of God will only rest upon us as we fulfill the divine purpose of our existence.

In no way does this imply an attitude of superiority or spiritual pride. God has need of many approaches in reaching people with truth and preparing them for His kingdom. There should be a variety of media programs emphasizing different aspects of truth. Each one can appeal to a different type of listener. All will not respond to the same kind of presentation. Amazing Facts is dedicated to restoring the old historic platform of doctrinal integrity and prophetic preaching. Our strong point is to uphold and proclaim the full gospel of salvation from the penalty and power of sin, and to do it without regard to the approval or disapproval of anyone except God.

Although the program was designed only for the Chesapeake area, requests began to pour in from other states asking for the broadcast. Quick revisions were made and new tapes prepared. Soon the radio log contained a list of almost a hundred stations across America including several powerful 50,000 watt stations from coast to coast.

For twenty years the Lord has led in the dramatic growth and success of the broadcast. Besides my own personal crusades, other evangelists have associated with us in the reaping crusades which bring hundreds to Christ every year. The staff now is composed of more than twenty workers, including several full-time evangelists.

Over twenty million of the Amazing Facts folders have been printed in the English language, besides the Danish, French, Spanish and Armenian editions. Within the area of Maryland and Delaware a careful record has determined that for every two people who complete the twelve-folder course, one person has been baptized as a result of the broadcast or folders.

With Amazing Facts aired at times on a hundred radio stations, and with personal crusades conducted in numerous large cities across the land, my life has been filled with more than the usual bitter-sweet of evangelism. There is great joy for the hundreds who accept the truth and heartache over those who reject it. Every converted life continues to amaze and delight me as God's grace-power performs His miracles before my very eyes.

19
Surgery by God

I must not forget to share with you how one of those recent miracles of God touched my own life in a very personal way. During the fall of 1970 my voice began to give out under the terrible constant strain of evangelism. For over six months there was an increasing hoarseness which made preaching almost a chore. At the end of my Thurmont series in August, it seemed utterly impossible that I could speak another night, yet I had a large campaign scheduled only a week later in Denver, Colorado.

I knew there was something seriously wrong with my vocal cords. Twice before, in Texas, I had developed ulcers on the cords due to heavy speaking engagements, and it seemed likely that the same problem had developed again. In each case a few weeks of absolute silence had remedied the condition completely. With little time to spare in case cancellations became necessary, I went to the highest medical authority in the area for consultations—Johns Hopkins University Hospital in Baltimore. Their throat specialists were the most highly acclaimed in the land, and they made a diagnosis which was confirmed by other independent specialists later—I had a nodule growing on my vocal cords which was causing the hoarseness. This time it was not an ulcer that would heal itself by silence. The Johns Hopkins specialists told me that surgery was the only alternative open to them. The growth would have to be removed by surgery.

My fears about cancer were allayed when the doctor assured me that he had never seen a vocal cord malignancy in a non-smoker. If I had smoked the chances were 50-50 that my voice box would have to be entirely removed. In answer to my further anxious questions, the doctor assured me that I could go ahead with the Denver campaign without making the condition worse, but there was absolutely no medication that could give any relief from the miserable hoarseness. Surgery was scheduled for the week following the close of the Denver crusade, and the next morning I reluctantly enplaned for the mile-high city. I didn't know how I could possibly preach for another three weeks, yet it was just as impossible to cancel the series when the opening sermon was scheduled that very night.

The first sermon in the beautiful Phipps Auditorium was a nightmare. The crowd was good, and the facilities were perfect, but I rasped and strained through the opening subject with misery to spare. It seemed to me that all my natural amplification had simply blown a fuse, and I was only going through the motions of preaching. Of course, it wasn't nearly so terrible to others as it seemed to me. I asked the audience to pray for my voice. I wanted to complete that crusade more than anything else in the world, but nothing seemed so humanly improbable.

The next morning I had to cancel another speaking appointment because I could only speak in a stage whisper at best. At noontime I confided to a fellow minister that I was finished unless God worked a miracle on my voice. I could not force myself to face another sermon. It hurt my throat to even whisper and I shuddered at the thought of preaching to that huge congregation of people. Fortunately, we were unable to obtain the hall for that second night, and I had a short respite, but the remainder of the three weeks was booked solid every night.

My friend was sympathetic. He had been doing a lot of praying, too, because if my voice failed he would have to take over the preaching. He finally said, "Look, Joe, I'm not going to tell you what to do, but I'd like to share with you what happened to me a short time ago." Then he proceeded to tell one of the most amazing stories I have ever heard. His tongue had developed a terrible sore which caused excruciating pain. He could hardly talk, eat or sleep, and the swelling and pain increased for three weeks while he sought medical help from doctor after doctor. Like the woman in the Bible, he "had suffered many things of many physicians . . . and was nothing bettered, but rather grew worse" (Mark 5:26).

Finally the doctors suggested that the ulcer might be cancerous and suggested taking a biopsy for lab study. The minister adamantly refused to allow any cutting of his tongue. At that point he decided to make a visit to a health food store operated by a dear little Christian lady who was reputed to know more about herbs and natural remedies than anybody else in the area. Along with the natural foods she had an abiding faith in God and the power of prayer.

Certainly it wasn't any medical knowledge that she possessed—perhaps it was just divine insight born of surrender to God—but after looking at his tongue, she said, "You have lead poisoning. You've been painting, haven't you?" My friend admitted that he had just recently been painting his kitchen. So she gave him 97 cents worth of herb teas and told him to take them for four days and the sore would be gone. And four days later he could not tell that his tongue had ever been sore.

"Now," the minister said, "I can take you to see this lady if you would like to go. I have nothing to urge." I said, "Let's go." For days I had been praying for God to heal my voice and to show me how to treat it. Now this suddenly seemed like the answer to those prayers. Within an hour we were walking into the health food store. It did not take me long to explain my problem. I held back nothing that the Johns Hopkins specialists had told me. I told her the surgery was set up, but I wanted her to please give me something to just relieve my voice for an hour each evening while I preached the Word. She looked at me kindly and said, "You are not going to have any surgery. God is going to heal your throat. I'm going to give you three things to take, and in three days your voice will be normal."

She gathered three different items from the shelves and explained to me how they should be taken hourly. Then she asked, "May I say a prayer for you?" Of course I agreed. She quietly bowed her head and asked God to heal my throat according to His will and grace. That was it. We thanked her and left. I went to my room and took the first of the natural medications she had given me. All evening I prayed earnestly that God would bless these simple remedies and manifest His mighty power. I went to bed with a sense of peace and assurance. The next morning I awoke and discovered to my great joy that my voice was almost normal. Only a slight huskiness remained, which gradually disappeared by the third day.

The crusade proceeded under the blessing of God and with no further speaking difficulty. I had perfect freedom in preaching and the Lord gave us many wonderful decisions for baptism. I knew the growth was gone from my vocal cords. Those three weeks were weeks of constant thanksgiving and heart-joy over the miracle God had worked. I knew that God had wrought through the simple things of nature to restore my voice! He had answered those many prayers in His own wonderful way, and I never ceased to ascribe the glory to Him for it. I do not believe for a moment that the medication of the little lady could have removed a nodule overnight that all the specialists could not even alleviate. Without the prayer, the faith, and the blessing of God the natural remedies would have fallen far short of that overnight miracle.

As soon as I returned to Baltimore I headed straight to Johns Hopkins Hospital to cancel the surgery date. The specialists looked at me in amusement when I announced to them that the growth was gone from my throat. They sprayed their numbing anesthetic on my tongue and soon had their little light focused on the vocal cords. They were astounded. They could not even locate where the nodule had been growing! One of them said, “You almost make a believer out of me.” They continued to marvel as I explained to them how God had taken the surgery out of their hands. One of them said, “We could never have assured you of the normal voice you have now if we had operated.” And you can be sure that my heart sang a little note higher in praise to God for doing it so much better in His own way.

20
No Survivors

Earlier in this book I marveled at the manner in which mighty consequences have hinged upon an almost incidental action. My life was saved twice during college days by the turn of a casual circumstance. Yet, of course, there was nothing casual about it. God works quietly behind the warp and woof of an infinitely complex life pattern. His plans are not frustrated by "unexpected" obstacles. The near tragedies of random circumstances may someday be viewed from the other side of the tapestry, and we will understand how divinely ordained the tiny details turned out to be.

Consider the mysterious, overruling providence which operated in my life on December 1, 1974. Just the day before, I had finished a very rewarding series of meetings in Newark, Ohio. Pastor Rima had driven me, under an overcast sky, the fifty miles to Columbus airport where I was to board a 10:00 a.m. flight into Washington, D.C.'s National Airport. Lu Ann was waiting for me there and the usual mixed feelings occupied my thoughts as I bade good-bye to Ohio friends and eagerly looked forward to being with my family again.

A month is a long time to be separated from loved ones, but when three crusades almost overlap, the time really begins to drag. No one could ever pay me in money to live out of a suitcase five or six months of each year. No offer of fabulous salary could influence me to do it. But twenty hours earlier I had watched the baptism of almost fifty precious souls who had responded to the call of God.

That was payday for me, and it brought to one hundred the number who had been led into the truth in Newark through Amazing Facts evangelism.

So it was with a great deal of gratitude and joy that I made my way past the electronic baggage scanner, and hurried toward the designated gate. Coming into the boarding area I noticed that most of the activity seemed to be taking place at the adjacent gate. Passengers were already crowding into line for boarding and the final call was being made over the intercom for TWA Flight 514 bound for National Airport in Washington.

Glancing at the overhead signs I noticed that Flight 514 was scheduled to leave at almost the same time as my reserved Eastern flight next door, and to arrive in Washington at the same time. Just then the speaker system crackled with the announcement that all passengers waiting to board my Eastern flight should expect at least a half hour delay before takeoff. My heart sank at the thought that Lu Ann would be kept waiting in Washington Airport. Then the thought flashed into my head that I could just as easily board the TWA flight at the next gate, and meet her at the appointed arrival time. Quickly I slipped into the end of the line and found myself moving rapidly toward the TWA counter.

Many times I had made last minute changes from one airline to another to meet a better schedule, and there was no apprehension on my part in doing so this time. But suddenly a possible problem occurred to me. At the large D.C. terminal Lu Ann would be waiting at the Eastern arrival gate, and I would have to go there to meet her. It could mean some wasted, anxious moments and even a possibility of not making contact. I stood uncertainly, weighing the decision, and watching the last man in front of me pass the ticket agent's counter. Then, on a last moment impulse, I drew back, put my ticket in my pocket, and walked back into the Eastern waiting area.

For some time I was disturbed and angry with myself that I had missed the opportunity to get home sooner on the other flight. It was one of those decisions which the mind can equally defend or reject, and after choosing to stay, all the arguments for going kept crowding into my head. I was still trying to put the whole thing out of my thinking when the boarding announcement was made forty minutes later.

The hour-long flight to Washington was uneventful, but the landing itself was the most frightening I have ever experienced. A terrible weather pattern had developed at the lower altitudes and the plane had to let down through tumultuous cross-winds gusting to fifty miles per hour. National Airport closed all its runways and directed all scheduled landings to either Dulles Airport or Baltimore. My plane was turned to the Baltimore Friendship Airport where we made a terrifying, vibrating descent with almost every passenger suffering from air-sickness. The TWA Flight 514 just ahead of us was directed to Dulles Airport in nearby suburban Virginia. We made it safely to the ground in spite of the buffeting winds, but Flight 514 didn't make it. The plane crashed into the top of a mountain in making its descent and all ninety-two people on board were killed. There were no survivors.

Fortunately I was able to reach Lu Ann by phone while she still waited anxiously at the other terminal. She had not heard of the fatal crash, and was thus spared much apprehension. But back in Newark there were hours of fearful waiting and praying before my friends received the word that I arrived safely. Knowing only that my plane was leaving at 10:00 a.m. they had every reason to believe that I was on the ill-fated TWA flight.

From a human viewpoint it was only an impulsive surge of emotional feeling that led me away from the TWA boarding area, but I know it was another demonstration of God's grace-power at work. Some of the greatest miracles in my life have pivoted upon the most humdrum circumstances. God works through the commonplace, and performs His wonders for the most undeserving. Not for a moment do I count myself more worthy of being spared than the ninety two who were killed. God's omniscient permissions cannot be understood by our poor minds. Someday He may permit my life to be taken in a similar manner, but now I can only believe that He gave me this gracious extension of life to use for His glory.

Often have I thought back upon the few moments when I watched the boarding line in the Columbus terminal. I knew none of them personally. They were just so many people, including the aged, the young and the infants. Totally unaware of approaching doom they laughed and chatted as they entered the plane. The last day of life had begun for them and they did not know it. Almost imperceptibly we are all edging toward that crucial day in our own lives when we will face the unexpected end. Jesus said, "Be ye also ready ... " And we need to be, every moment of every day. I do not know what the future holds or in which direction God's wonderful will may direct my life. But I am convinced that nobody in the world has a more thrilling or exciting work than God has assigned me. To meet thousands of people all across these United States who trace their spiritual interests to Amazing Facts and see hundreds of them step out to be baptized in our public crusades is surely the most joyful and fulfilling experience one could know.

My life has been punctuated with conflicts, tragedy

and danger. Yet God has overruled to turn those crises into reservoirs of spiritual grace and power. Looking back, I can already discern some of the reasons for God's providential permissions in my past. As for the experiences which still seem mysterious, I trust the God whose hand has been over me for good.

Epilogue

Amazing Facts has prospered under the grace of God ever since its first radio broadcast from Baltimore, Maryland, in 1966. The late Joe Crews was speaker and director for more than 30 years, leading the ministry with the Holy Spirit's influence to become a multifaceted, worldwide outreach changing lives with simple, straightforward Bible teaching.

When Joe Crews suddenly died in 1994, the ministry's workers and friends were shocked and deeply saddened. But as he had always been, Joe was already prepared for the next step. Before his tragic death, he had searched for and found another willing servant to take the ministry's reins and guide it into the 21st century.

With his direct and compassionate presentations, Pastor Doug Batchelor has since become one of America's best loved evangelists, drawing on the trusted, Bible-based legacy established by founder Joe Crews. Amazing Facts remains a truly well-respected leader in drawing the lost to Jesus and enabling them to reach others.

The heartbeat of the gospel pulsating from Amazing Facts is heard, seen, and read today by millions across the globe. *Bible Answers Live*, a popular call-in radio show hosted by Doug Batchelor, and *Joe Crews Classics* reach thousands of radio listeners each day with direct Bible answers to people's most difficult questions.

On television, the *Everlasting Gospel* and *Millennium of Prophecy* is being broadcast to every corner of the globe, and are some America's most popular and trusted sources of Bible truth. Currently, Amazing Facts media ministry is on more than 100 television stations and 11 satellite and cable networks throughout the United States, Europe, Australia, Central and South America, the Middle East, and Asia.

These powerful radio and television gospel outlets are supported by a robust publishing ministry that offers thousands of resources every day, including its own leading materials on Christian doctrine and living for believers and seekers alike. In addition, the ministry has reached a whole new audience online with user-friendly, gospel-teaching websites at www.amazingfacts.org and www.BibleUniverse.com.

And of course, Amazing Facts still harnesses the successful ministries Joe Crews helped create to reach souls for Christ. The correspondence Bible School reaches tens of thousands each year with colorful, detailed, and thought-provoking Study Guides. Going yet one step further, the ministry has now made these exciting evangelistic studies available online and offers the new, innovative *Storacles of Prophecy* at BibleUniverse.

Amazing Facts soul-winning live evangelistic series continue to reap a bountiful harvest for the kingdom, with more than 60 seminars each year featuring compelling presentations, Bible-based reasoning, and caring evangelists. This mainstay from the Joe Crews' years is still one of the most effective ways to reach people searching for truth.

With the solid foundation laid by God-led Joe Crews, the new dynamic vision of Pastor Doug Batchelor, the heartfelt prayers and sacrificial support of ministry friends, and most important, the guidance of the Lord, Amazing Facts is poised to carry the gospel deep into the future in preparation for the soon coming of Jesus Christ.

"Someday soon, when Jesus comes, the woven pattern of my life may be seen from both sides of the loom; tears will no longer distort the view, and I have every confidence that I shall thank the dear Lord Jesus face-to-face for holding the reins on my life and permitting the circumstances to be exactly as they were. In the meantime, I rejoice in the love of God who has now allowed my lot to be cast in such pleasant places. The truth grows sweeter every day, and the light grows brighter up ahead as we approach the blessed day of His appearing. 'Even so, come, Lord Jesus.'"

—Joe Crews, founder of Amazing Facts Ministries.

AMAZING FACTS

Visit us online at
www.amazingfacts.org
and check out our online catalog
filled with other great books, videos,
CDs, audiotapes, and more!

Don't miss our FREE online
Bible Prophecy course at
www.bibleuniverse.com
Enroll today and
expand your universe!